Brothers, Sing On!

Brothers, Sing On!

A History of Pontarddulais Male Choir (1960-2010)

Eric Jones

y Lolfa

ISBN: 978 184771 2325

Published, printed and bound in Wales
by Y Lolfa Cyf., Talybont, Ceredigion SY24 5HE
website www.ylolfa.com
e-mail ylolfa@ylolfa.com
tel 01970 832 304
fax 832 782

CONTENTS

ACKNOWLEDGEMENTS

So NUMEROUS HAVE BEEN the administrative officers of Côr Meibion Pontarddulais over its fifty years of existence, that it is impossible to acknowledge them all by name. Yet, I am greatly in their debt with regards the consultation of source material in preparation for this book. In particular a succession of conscientious secretaries have diligently kept minutes of meetings, copies of correspondence, concert programmes, itineraries of all kinds, and a host of other documentary evidence delineating what the choir has done and achieved since 1960. Inevitably this wealth of material has ended up in a very large number of files and boxes in the safe-keeping of the present day secretary, Lyn Anthony. There is little doubt that I have tested his patience to the extreme, but his tolerance and stoicism in the face of my frequently impatient requests, coupled with his healthy sense of humour, have all helped to make my task that much easier.

A small sub-committee of four was established by the choir to oversee plans for the fiftieth anniversary celebrations. I am very grateful indeed to my three colleagues on that committee, John Davies, Alun Davies and Winston Price, all distinguished servants of the choir, for their interest and encouragement as the writing of this book progressed. I am particularly grateful to John Davies for reading the typesrcipt of this book and for making valuable suggestions.

I would also like to express my thanks to the many individuals who have spared time to talk to me at length about their memories and recollections. These have included past and present choristers, choir friends and supporters, as well as individuals associated with other choirs.

I have been able to consult two published historical records pertaining to the choir. John Davies wrote his *Chronicled History 1960–1972* as a contribution to publicity before one of the choir's overseas tours in 1973. Professor

Ieuan Williams's *Côr Meibion Pontarddulais* was written as a contribution to the choir's twenty fifth anniversary in 1985. The preparation of my biography of Noel Davies, *Maestro*, meant amassing a great deal of valuable material that has naturally been equally relevant and useful in the preparation of this book. In that respect I wish to thank Gillian Evans for allowing me extended access to Noel Davies's papers, bequeathed to her following her godfather's death.

As preparation for elements of Chapter 6 it was vital to elicit the views of the present-day membership of the choir. Their one hundred per cent response to a detailed questionnaire proved most valuable, and I sincerely thank each and every one of them. In terms of the same chapter, my daughter Luned brought her professional expertise to bear in helping her father with statistical analyses and diagrams, for which I am extremely grateful. My wife, Gwen, has also been the usual tower of strength, reading proofs, making constructive comments and helping with photographs. Thanks also go to Meinir for her encouragement during the writing process, and for the frequent tidying of her father's often dishevelled papers and cluttered desk.

My thanks also go to the present musical director, Clive Phillips, for his interest and support. Founder conductor, Noel Davies, has, sadly, not lived to witness the choir's fiftieth anniversary. He would have been very proud of the continuing successes of the choir, and I can only hope that my old friend would be content with this celebratory volume.

Finally, I wish to acknowledge my appreciation of the guidance and wise counsel of the staff at Y Lolfa publishers, and to thank them for overseeing the progress of this volume through the press with minimal stress for the author. In this respect I am particularly indebted to Eirian Jones.

Any opinions expressed herein are of course my own, and it goes without saying that I am solely responsible for any errors of fact that still remain in the text.

PREFACE

BEARING IN MIND THE particularly rich history of our musical heritage as a nation, surprisingly little has been written about it – all the more ironic when we consider that we have two native languages at our disposal. There have of course been notable and distinguished exceptions, particularly in more recent decades, with the meticulous academic research and enlightening publications of David Allsobrook, Lyn Davies and Gareth Williams, for example, proving invaluable contributions in this respect. Male choirs have been an important part of that musical landscape, and yet a written record of the history of any one of them is a rare thing indeed. Again, thankfully, there have been notable exceptions including, for example, Dean Powell's pictorial history, *Treorchy Male Choir*, in the 'Images of Wales' series. Books on male choirs in general are also scarce, with the recent publication of Meurig Owen's *North Wales Male Voice Choirs* a very welcome addition.

Music in Wales, a symposium edited by Peter Crossley-Holland, was published in 1948 as a general introduction to the musical life of Wales at that time. The chapter entitled 'The Choral Tradition' was written by W R Allen, then a lecturer in music at the University of Wales, Aberystwyth. Of the male choir tradition he wrote:

> A number of choirs are of a specialised nature. Male choirs are numerous, for instance, like those at Dowlais and Morriston.

'Specialised' and 'numerous' they may have been, but that was it. There was apparently no more to be said, and they were dismissed in two sentences!

There may well have been a decline in the number of Welsh male choirs in the intervening years, but there are at least seventy male choirs in Wales today who have established their own websites, many of which, incidentally, are particularly sophisticated. There are presumably many more active male choirs in Wales who have not yet quite caught up with the technological revolution. Even estimating only modest average membership numbers, there are still many thousands of gentlemen singing in our male choirs and continuing to contribute to our contemporary musical scene as a nation. Let us not forget either that there are innumerable 'Welsh exile' male choirs who are active in many countries across the globe.

As part of its fiftieth anniversary celebrations in 2010, Côr Meibion Pontarddulais decided that the publication of a chronicle of its history was to be an important element. This book, then, is a small contribution to what is sadly a limited body of literature about our male choral tradition. It is a story covering fifty years of music-making by one choir of men. It is the story of one choir's unique contribution to the nation's musical heritage. It hopefully sees beyond the music too, for the story is not entirely a musical one. The distinguished English musician and writer, and one time enthusiastic fan of Côr Meibion Pontarddulais, the late Percy M Young wrote the following in his admirable book, *The Choral Tradition*:

> I have had much pleasure in and understanding from choral music. From long experience in it I have, I think, learned more about the nature and purpose of music as a whole than in any other way. I have, too, learned a great deal about people.

He was emphasising that there is a social context to all music making, and yet there is something extra special about choral music, bringing in its wake a sense of community. The question 'Why do we sing?' is an interesting but unanswerable one, as we sing in the most conflicting of emotional circumstances. We sing at celebrations and at bereavements; at the chapel and in the pub; in the concert hall and at the rugby match; we sing in sorrow and in joy. This is a story of music-making interwoven with the cloth of life itself, of ordinary members of the community who discovered music as a necessary means of expression through a highly disciplined and creative team activity. They discovered through their endeavours a sense of promise and optimism, with the individual bringing something of value to the whole. They also discovered that singing together helped them connect with each other and to their environment. It is an activity that has always bonded people throughout the generations, and one that has maintained its capability of generating a certain 'feel-good factor'.

But of course, the story is more than about what singing together in a choir brings to the individual chorister. As in the case of any group of musicians, a choir's primary function is to communicate with a listening audience. It is a refined musical 'instrument' that transforms the fruits of the imagination of composers and musical arrangers into audible entities and conveys them on the concert platform, or through mechanical reproduction of one kind or another. It would be pure conjecture to speculate on how many people have heard Côr Meibion Pontarddulais sing 'live' over its fifty years of existence. How many more will have experienced the sound of the choir through the medium of radio and television, record, tape and disc? And how much of their music may have touched the innermost feelings of those listeners?

There is also a philanthropic and altruistic dimension to the choir's story that ought not to be forgotten. In the same way as it is impossible to estimate how many people have heard the choir sing, it is equally elusive to estimate how many charitable organisations have benefited from its services over a period of half a century. The vast majority of concerts have been performed with the admirable aim of raising funds for a wide variety of good causes, up and down the country and abroad too. Who can estimate the vast sums of money raised through the choir's beneficence?

It was Ella Fitzgerald who said, 'The only thing better than singing is more singing'. This is also the sentiment behind the title of this book. Known originally as *Sangerhilsen* in Norwegian, *Brothers Sing On* is the title of a short unaccompanied setting for male choir by Edvard Grieg, of a poem by the composer's compatriot Sigurd Skavlan. It was introduced into the repertoire of Côr Meibion Pontarddulais during the choir's tenth anniversary year, and the title was often quoted by the choir's founding conductor, Noel Davies, as an exhortation to his choristers to maintain standards. It seemed an appropriate title for this celebratory book as an encouragement to the choristers, the choir's administrators and musical team, at a time of looking back with pride, to move forward again with confidence and commitment.

The traditional chronological approach has been taken here, with the exception of a chapter devoted to the way that the choir, despite its international status, has never forgotten its Welsh identity and roots. Having argued linguistically that the bulk of the book should be in English in order to serve and reach a wider audience, it may appear something of a paradox to have written that particular chapter in Welsh. However, it seemed the natural thing to do.

Eric Jones, July 2010

1

THE FIRST DECADE
(1960–70)

IN HIS ADMIRABLE BOOK, *Hanes Pontarddulais* (A History of Pontarddulais), E Lewis Evans described the majority of Pontarddulais residents in the last quarter of the nineteenth century as 'Cymry oddi cartref yn gwneud cân'. It is a reference to the fact that the town had by then experienced an influx of migrant workers and their families, mainly from other south Wales valleys, attracted by work at the rapidly developing tinplate works and local collieries. The Welsh epithet's reference to song clearly indicates that the newcomers came from a background of strong cultural roots, particularly so in terms of music. This is important in the context of this book, for it was from such a community, with Welsh as its first language and a strong Christian ethos, that a remarkable lineage of musical organisations sprang. This is the story of one of them – Côr Meibion Pontarddulais, the Pontarddulais Male Choir, now celebrating its fiftieth anniversary, and acclaimed internationally as one of the world's outstanding male choirs.

Pontarddulais and its environs are steeped in historical significance on several counts. There is evidence of ancient earthworks; the Romans have left their mark; the local marshes were home to the medieval Llandeilo Talybont church, now demolished and completely and authentically rebuilt at the Sain Ffagan Folk Museum, Cardiff, as it had stood in the sixteenth century; and some of the most significant events during the turmoil of the Rebecca riots took place in the area too. Such historical detail has been eloquently chronicled in Lewis Evans's book, as well as in *Bont: the story of a village and its rugby club* by Denver Evans, and in *Images of Pontarddulais down the years* by John Miles. Valuable contributions by local historians Gwyn Griffiths, Ivor Griffiths and others can be accessed on the internet.

However, as far as this story is concerned, it is the cultural history of the town from towards the end of the nineteenth century and onwards to the first half of the twentieth that will give a clear focus as to the background and circumstances that helped establish an environment in which a new youthful choir could begin to flourish in the 1960s.

By the 1880s Pontarddulais had already witnessed a proliferation of chapel building, designed to house large congregations. Unsurprisingly, a significant number of the town's cultural activities were centred on, and greatly influenced by them. Each of the main chapels had its own choir; the gymanfa ganu was at the height of its popularity; competitive concerts were held in Gopa chapel and the Pontarddulais Eisteddfod took place every Boxing Day. In 1882 the Market and Public Hall was built in Hendy, becoming established as a venue for many concerts. Two years later, the 'United Choir' was formed, with members of the chapel choirs combining to sing large-scale works. Not all cultural innovations were chapel based however, and this decade also saw the establishment of the Pontarddulais Amateur Christy Minstrels who gave popular light concerts modelled on similar shows in the USA, accompanied by some kind of *ad hoc* band. The first Pontarddulais Brass Band was also established at this time, as well as several fife and drum bands.

The 1890s saw the establishment of a reading circle, ultimately named 'The Pontarddulais Mechanics Institute'. The special building housing the circle's meetings, also known as the 'Institute' was erected in 1906, and became the home of a diverse array of cultural activities over the following decades and up to the present day. The area also had its creative literati, and in 1901 there was great rejoicing and a series of parades when Gwili – the Reverend John Gwili Jenkins of Hendy – won the coveted National crown at the age of 29. At the same National Eisteddfod in Merthyr, Rhymney were the victors in the male choir competition. There was evidently a 'Pontarddulais Male Choir' in being at the time, as records indicate that at the Merthyr Eisteddfod they trailed behind in sixth place out of seven choirs – hardly an auspicious prophecy of what was to come several decades later.

Gwili was the librettist for the cantata *Llyn y Fan*, first performed at the Swansea National Eisteddfod of 1907. The composer was David Vaughan Thomas, a prodigious talent whose parents had moved to Pontarddulais when he was a child. Thomas, after studying mathematics at Exeter College, Oxford, turned his attention to music and taught for a period at Harrow School before returning to Wales. He became one of Wales's leading composers, and some of his song settings are strikingly original. After settling once more in the Swansea area, he was to exert considerable influence on musical matters in Pontarddulais, particularly as conductor of the formidable choral society.

If anything, developments intensified over coming decades, particularly in terms of the number of various musical groups. A male singing party was established in Hendy in 1910 eventually developing into the 'Hendy Choral Society' and a new Pontarddulais Silver Band appeared in 1914. The 'Great War' inevitably took its toll, but the 1920s witnessed a new intensity of activity. A Glandulais

Male Choir and a Pontarddulais Ladies Choir continued to give weekly concerts as did the Siloh Augmented Orchestra, which later formed the nucleus of the Pontarddulais Orchestra. The Ladies Choir was accompanied by Annie Grey Rees who, years later was to conduct the youth choir, also somewhat confusingly called Côr Glandulais. In the 1920s there was also a Cwmbach Male Choir, thus named because most of the members lived in the Cwmbach area of Upper Mill. It may well be with so many choral groups in being, that finding new and appropriate names was becoming something of a challenge. The Glandulais Male Choir somewhat arrogantly changed its name to 'The Welsh Premiers' as they became the first local organisation to take part in a radio broadcast in 1926.

At this time the Pontarddulais Choral Society recast itself as the Pontarddulais Operatic Society, with the youthful T Haydn Thomas, nephew of D Vaughan Thomas, taking the helm and giving a performance of *The Pirates of Penzance* in 1923. The operatic society soon reverted to being a choral society once again, and entered the competitive field, gaining a second place at the Llanelli National Eisteddfod in 1930 and winning two years later at Port Talbot. In the 1920s Haggar's Picturedome, originally a skating rink and known locally as 'The Rink' became the venue for many concerts, and had its own repertory company. The so-called 'Gym' had also been a venue for concerts before later becoming a cinema.

The Dan Mathews Drama Company had its roots in Trinity chapel, gaining considerable momentum during the early years of the century and ultimately forging a national reputation as paramount in the world of Welsh-language drama. Originally known as 'Cwmni y Ddôl' and later as the 'Dulais Dramatic Society', its influence led to the formation of as many as seven drama companies in Pontarddulais in the 1930s. Later in the field of drama, the Berwyn Players also developed a fine reputation. The art of recitation also grew in importance, again with Dan Mathews as teacher and instructor of individuals and groups, followed later by the talented Ceinwen Smith Owen.

After the Second World War, another Pontarddulais Male Choir flourished between 1945 and 1952, presumably following the demise of its competitively ill-fated predecessor. This new choir was conducted by local schoolmaster Levi Hopkin, who was subsequently to direct the afore mentioned mixed youth choir, Côr Glandulais, itself an addition to other youth and school choirs in the town. In 1949, the latest in a line of fine brass bands, the Pontarddulais Town Band, was formed.

Thus we arrive at the 1950s, and before we examine exactly what was going on musically during this decade in Pontarddulais, significant social change affecting its people merits attention in order to establish a context for what was to happen culturally in the forthcoming years. The tinplate works – major employers of the local workforce since the nineteenth century – began to close down one by one, as the large new tinplate plants at Trostre and Felindre, opened to replace the old style works, came into their own. Some of the old works were taken over by light industries, but jobs within the town became significantly fewer as collieries also went into decline, though the mine at Graig Merthyr remained productive. Pontarddulais began to experience unemployment, with most of those who were in work having to travel outside the town itself. The railway line from Swansea to Pontarddulais eventually closed down in the 1960s, and though the mid Wales line remained open, the substantial station buildings, platforms, sheds and yards, so important in terms of freight as well as passengers over the years, were eventually demolished, and the significant influence of the railway on the town dwindled virtually to nothing. The community was changing, and traditional values were under threat. There was a noticeable decline in the use of the Welsh language, and a decline also in attendance at the chapels and churches, with a resulting shift of cultural activities away from the religious strongholds of the past.

Cultural roots, particularly musical ones, were deep and held firm, and though the number of groups inevitably declined, Côr Glandulais continued to go from strength to strength, and the brass band had by this time established a national reputation. The Pontarddulais Choral Society, affectionately known as the 'Côr Mawr' and still under the assured and incisive direction of the remarkable T Haydn Thomas, was at the peak of its considerable reputation. On no fewer than eleven occasions, the choir was invited to perform extended choral works with professional orchestras at the Swansea Festival of Music under distinguished conductors such as Adrian Boult, Nicolai Malko, Hugo Rignold and John Barbirolli at the city's impressive Brangwyn Hall. At several of these concerts the choir also gave first performances of large-scale works by contemporary Welsh composers such as Daniel Jones, Arwel Hughes and Ian Parrott. This choir was at its majestic best and represented the national élite of amateur music-making bodies of that era, and it was Pontarddulais based.

In contrast, at the local youth club, youngsters were beginning to develop and refine their vocal skills, albeit in a comparatively modest way, under the enthusiastic encouragement of a young teacher recently returned to the area. The son of a coalminer, and born and brought up a stone's throw from Pontarddulais in the little village of Grovesend, Noel Davies was steeped in the musical tradition of Gowerton Boys' Grammar School as a former double bass player in the school's impressive orchestra, and his mother sang in T Haydn's 'Côr Mawr'. As the assistant warden at the youth club with responsibility for musical activities, he formed a male singing group, another for ladies, and combined them to form a mixed choir. He also established an orchestra there. The choirs prepared for the occasional concert and 'Noson Lawen' but more importantly they worked hard to compete at the Glamorgan Youth Eisteddfod held annually in Porthcawl, and at the National Eisteddfod too. The Festival Shield at the Youth Eisteddfod, awarded to the club with the highest number of marks in stage events, went to Pontarddulais for a remarkable seven years in succession at this time, and there was a first place for the mixed youth choir at the Ebbw Vale National in 1958 and a second place two years later at Cardiff.

The club catered for youngsters from the age of 15 to 21, and with the dawn of the 1960s a contingent of members began to realise that their time at the youth centre was coming to an end. However, their enthusiasm for music, and choral singing in particular, was not to diminish; there were after all two successful mixed choirs within the town, both of which were anxious to recruit new and younger members. Having experienced the thrill and rich sounds of close harmony as a male group in the youth club, the young men began to contemplate the possibility of abandoning their female counterparts and forming a male voice party on a trial basis. In their innocent naivety, they probably knew nothing of the historical precedents – a good thing, bearing in mind that the first male choir from the town had been humbled at the Merthyr National Eisteddfod in 1901. They may well have known little or nothing either about the Pontarddulais Male Choir established after the war by Levi Hopkin, when they, after all, had been only little children in the primary school. In any event, a plan was hatched, fully endorsed by Noel Davies, to establish a party of male singers to meet independently of the youth club and to rehearse on a different evening. Unsurprisingly, their mentor, whom they already idolised, was invited to conduct.

What were the qualities that had endeared Noel Davies to his young charges? No doubt they recognised his diffidence and unassuming nature as well as his total dedication and boundless enthusiasm. They would have appreciated his innate musicality and his determination to achieve high standards of performance. More than anything though, they valued his genuine interest in them as individual young people. Whilst a student at Gowerton's Sixth Form, Noel Davies had been required to leave school before completing his studies in order to undertake his National Service in the Royal Navy. He served as a clerk for two years at Devonport before returning home and moving on to Coleg Harlech – 'Coleg yr ail gyfle' – the 'College of the second chance'. There he was influenced by national figures of stature such as Dan Harry, D Tecwyn Lloyd and Meredydd Evans, individuals immersed in Welsh culture, keen, in the words of a college publicity pamphlet of 1947, 'to help potential leaders in the life of local communities to develop their latent powers and to increase their capacity for service.' In order to gain a teaching qualification, he went on to Trinity College Carmarthen, where he became the president of the Student Representative Council, and came under the influence of another great Welsh academic, Jac L Williams.

His first teaching post was at Stourbridge Road Primary School in Halesowen, Worcestershire, though he returned to Wales a year later to a post at Tonyrywen Primary School, Cardiff. In 1954 he was appointed music teacher at the Pontarddulais Secondary Modern School where he had himself been a pupil for a brief period before moving on to Gowerton. The Secondary Modern school was also the venue for meetings of the Pontarddulais Youth Club. With his wife, Joan, he settled to live in Garden Village, Kingsbridge, Gorseinon, where he remained for the rest of his life.

With about two dozen youngsters in attendance, and Noel Davies to guide them, a meeting of so called 'augmented youth choir members' took place on 19 October 1960. Key decisions included the nomination of Noel Davies as conductor, with W Frank Thomas elected as secretary and Alun J Rees as treasurer. Gareth Davies and Philip Jones made up the remainder of this embryonic committee, and choristers were given a week to come up with an appropriate name for the fledgling choir. They responded ambitiously with 'Côr Meibion Pontarddulais, Pontarddulais Male Voice Choir' (adjusting the English version some eight years later to 'Pontarddulais Male Choir'). At this second meeting local police officer Gareth Davies was elected the first chairman in a distinguished and industrious line, and the formulation of rules and regulations of governance began, one of which stated:

> A levy of 6d [2½p] per week be made on each member of the Choir and committee, excluding the Conductor, irrespective of whether the member is at practice or not. If a member is not at practice then he is expected to pay the full amount owing when he next attends.

In order to avoid any clash with youth club meetings – as Noel Davies continued to work there – rehearsals for the new male choir were to take place on Wednesday evenings at the secondary school. The purchase of music copies was expedited by the donation of eight guineas [£8.40] by the former youth club members. Committee meetings proliferated over succeeding weeks and on 9 November it was decided to invite Ieuan M Williams, then Director of Extra Mural Studies at the University of Wales, Swansea, to become the choir's first president. Born and bred in Pontarddulais and a former pupil and later master at Gowerton Boys' Grammar School, he gladly accepted and remained as president until his death in 2000.

Another Gowertonian, Bryan Llewellyn, was appointed

the first accompanist, and by early 1961, reflecting the steady growth in numbers, additional members were added to the committee. A second weekly rehearsal, on a Sunday evening, commenced at the Mechanics Institute on 19 February. After all, it was essential to build a worthy repertoire as invitations began to arrive asking the choir to perform in public. Côr Meibion Pontarddulais gave its first concert on 18 February 1961 at the somewhat inauspicious venue of the Memorial Hall at Garnswllt, a small hamlet on the outskirts of Pontarddulais. The performance was deemed a success and a youthful Gwyndaf Jones was thereafter appointed deputy conductor and vice chairman, and the choir embarked on a series of eleven further concerts during that first year of music making. They were all within Pontarddulais and the surrounding area, reflecting the choir's aspiration to root itself within a supporting local community, and to begin making its own contribution to the immensely rich cultural heritage of the locality. The repertoire was initially safe and conservative, gradually adding to the hymn-tune and folk song arrangements already mastered at the youth club. However, there was already a commitment on the part of the conductor to expand the repertoire in line with the musical development and maturity of the choir.

The most local of eisteddfodau was the one held annually at the Loughor Welfare Hall, and it was here that Côr Meibion Pontarddulais ventured to the competitive field for the first time. Their only opponents were the Dunvant Male Choir, one of the longest established and most experienced male choirs in Wales. The result was an inevitable victory for Dunvant who, in a magnanimous gesture of good will and encouragement shared their prize money with their young rivals. On its next competitive venture, singing in the early hours of the morning at the Seven Sisters Eisteddfod on 3 June 1961, the choir was to come third out of three. Older residents of Pontarddulais recalled the fate of another Pontarddulais Male Choir at the Merthyr National Eisteddfod of 1901. The omens were not good!

During that first year the choir had grown to over ninety members with some older and more experienced singers having joined the ranks, although the average age was still remarkably only 26. Early disappointments counted for nothing as Noel Davies took his troops to the prestigious Miners' Eisteddfod at Porthcawl in the autumn, and a competition that had attracted twelve leading choirs. Previous omens were indeed ignored as the new young choir came in third behind the victors, the famous 'Ferndale Imperial' and second placed 'Rhymney Silurian'. This experience was an undoubted boost to morale and acted as a springboard to greater things.

Musically, the first year had been a success, mainly because of the very firm foundations established for future progress and advancement. In terms of administration and structure, the young officers and committee members were gradually finding their feet, putting into place appropriate procedures, initially in a somewhat *ad hoc* manner as needs arose. Matters of fundamental importance were nevertheless dealt with, one of which had on it the clear stamp of Noel Davies. On all musical issues, the conductor had the last word; there would be no discussion on what to sing, very little on where to perform, and none at all on how. Without being heavy handed, discipline was appropriately strict. Regular attendance at rehearsal was paramount; there was a plan to fix the position of each chorister in practices as far as this was possible; smoking was allowed only during the half time break, and then well outside the rehearsal room; and there was to be no unauthorised singing in the official name of the choir.

Social intercourse was not to be neglected, and the first official dinner was held during the Christmas period of

1960 at the Boar's Head in Carmarthen, with the first dinner dance held in September 1961 at the Pier Hotel, Mumbles. Financially, the original levy on members had been adjusted to 2/6 [12½p] per calendar month, with an additional weekly sweepstake of 6d [2½p] per ticket, with proceeds shared between the winner and the choir. Acknowledging the difficult economic climate of the day and the plight of the unemployed, 'non-earners' were only required to contribute a shilling [5p] a month. The treasurer's report at the first Annual General Meeting on 11 October 1961 showed a surplus of income over expenditure of £179. Musically and financially the choir was already on a strong footing, and looking to the future with confidence.

Still unexplained to this day, the young choir, hardly known at this stage even within the confines of south Wales, received an unexpected invitation to sing at the prestigious Bromsgrove Festival in the English Midlands during the early summer of 1962. They made the most of their opportunity and delighted the audience with their youthful exuberance in an evening of 'Celtic music'. It was on this occasion that the choir uniform, at least in part, was worn for the first time. With little regard for tradition, the choir had decided to forego the usual formal evening dress associated with male choirs, and had plumped for an uniform comprising a striking green blazer with grey trousers. The newly designed tie and blazer badge were not quite ready for the Bromsgrove event, and choristers wore the Gowerton Grammar School tie at the concert, a decision that reflected the close connection of so many members with that particular educational establishment. As befitted the occasion though, conductor and accompanist wore full evening dress. Bryan Llewellyn by this time had taken up a teaching post in England, and the mantle of accompanist had fallen on another old Gowertonian in Elwyn Sweeting, a dedicated servant to the choir for the next six years.

The National Eisteddfod of 1962 was to be held close to home at Llanelli, and Noel Davies's courageous decision to compete immediately led to a significant problem. The 'Chief' competition was reserved for those choirs with over eighty voices, whereas the 'Second' competition was for those with fewer choristers in their ranks. Numbers had increased significantly within the Pontarddulais Choir, but by the early May closing date for entries there was no guarantee that the choir could in fact stage over eighty voices at the August eisteddfod. Consequently it was decided to compete in the 'Second' male choir competition. Recruitment continued unabated though, with membership topping a hundred in the weeks leading up to the eisteddfod, and there was no alternative other than to put in place a selection procedure based on attendance at rehearsals. The two demanding test pieces were 'Y Ffoadur' by Tawe Jones, and 'De Profundis' by Vincent Thomas, and the competition was a momentous and lengthy one involving no less than thirteen choirs. Bearing in mind the considerable experience of the other choirs, the second place gained by the Bont was truly remarkable, and the cause of great celebration. They were, after all, the runners up to the renowned Silurian Singers conducted by the indomitable Glynne Jones. Having comfortably crossed the numbers threshold, Pontarddulais were well aware that at the following year's National, were they to enter, they would compete in the 'Chief' event, and could possibly come up against Glynne Jones's other celebrated choir, Pendyrus.

The year 1962 was also significant for the staging of the choir's first annual concert, a similar event having proved impossible to organise the previous year. Now though, following the growth of a sufficiently substantial repertoire, and an increasingly confident administrative regime, preparations proceeded with gusto. The venue was to be the newly refurbished Welfare Hall, previously the Tivoli Cinema – central in terms of the community, but painfully inadequate on several counts. Though now officially designated as a 'hall', it still had the feel of a cinema. Dark and somewhat cramped, the stage was inadequate in size for what was now a very large body of men, and the restricted seating capacity for the audience necessitated the rationing of tickets for choristers' friends and families. Such inadequacies were roundly ignored, and a stoic determination to make the most of a special occasion prevailed. The concert took place on Sunday 9 December with professional guest artistes Kenneth Langabeer, tenor, and the Swansea born soprano Mary Thomas, the first two of a stunning array of star-studded singers who were to perform at subsequent annual concerts over the years.

Further adjustments in subscription fees reflected the gradually changing age profile of the membership. The monthly levy was abandoned and those in full employment were now asked for an annual contribution of one guinea [£1.05]; the fee for a full-time student was 7/6d [37½p] and nothing was expected of senior citizens. It was at this time also that a flourishing Ladies' Section was formed, primarily for the purpose of fund raising and the preparation of refreshments at various events, with its first task being the provision of finance for the purchase of the new blazer badges. The women's liberation movement had not yet manifested itself.

The badge had been cleverly designed by Alun Rees, the choir's treasurer, and was a subtle amalgam of three elements: the daffodil, the Welsh national emblem; the trio of ravens that formed an important element of the coat of arms of the Llwchwr Urban District Council, and finally an image of the old church of Llandeilo Talybont, mentioned earlier in this chapter. The inscription heralded the Welsh-language version of the choir's name, Côr Meibion Pontarddulais.

Early 1963 saw the choir suffer a significant blow in terms of its administrative personnel with the resignation through ill health of the first secretary and founding member, Frank Thomas. His high level of organisational skill had proved crucial from the outset, and he would be sorely missed. Sadly, he was never able to return to the choir fold as his health gradually deteriorated, and he passed away in April 1964.

Donald White's first responsibility as the new secretary in 1963 was to help oversee the creation of the choir's constitution as a first formal document of substance and authority. On the musical front, activity intensified as the choir's first appearance in the 'Chief Male Voice' competition at the National Eisteddfod loomed. The long journey to Llandudno was a tedious one with the sleeping arrangements on camp beds in a local school hardly conducive to a top class performance. But the youngsters of the choir together with the older stalwarts were made of stern stuff, and they triumphed in glorious fashion. The victory, however, was not without controversy. Only two choirs had entered for the competition, the other being the famous and formidable Pendyrus. The test pieces were 'Salm Bywyd' by the Llanelli born composer Haydn Morris, and a setting of the 'Agnus Dei' by Jacob Kerle, a Flemish composer of the renaissance period, to be sung, incidentally, in Latin. Not only did the result come as something of a shock to some, but also the winning margin of thirteen points was truly astonishing. Adjudicators were criticised in the national press, whilst some commentators expressed the view that the Bont victory would prove 'a flash in the pan'. They were wrong!

The young choir had certainly caused a stir. They now numbered over 120 singers and the average age was still only thirty. Invitations arrived for engagements of the kind that they had only dreamed of previously. As winners at the Llandudno National they appeared on network BBC television for the first time on 25 October in a programme entitled *Goreuon yr Ŵyl*. A month later they travelled by train to give their first ever performance in London at a Moral Re-armament Association conference, entertaining a host of international delegates at the Westminster Theatre, after which they lunched at the home of Lady Margaret Barrett, grand-daughter of David Lloyd George. As is the case with any group of musicians, recording their performances is undoubtedly the most appropriate and effective way of capturing for posterity the essence of their musicianship, and thus the cutting of the first disc was a significant event in the history of the choir. This was an extended-play record produced by Welsh Teldisc Records, a company whose director John Edwards contributed significantly to Welsh music at this time, so much so that following his untimely death, the Guild for the Promotion of Welsh Music established its highest honour in his memory. The two recorded pieces were Maldwyn Price's 'Crossing the Plain', these days considered somewhat politically incorrect, but still sung, and Pugh Evans's 'Y Delyn Aur'. Edwards enthused eloquently on the record sleeve:

> Noel Davies, the young conductor, has built a youthful choir around himself to provide a freshness of sound, which is very impressive. The Pontarddulais Choir is a new star on the horizon in Wales and it brings a new interest to the Male Voice movement. It now takes its place with the established choirs Treorchy, the most famous of them all, Rhosllanerchrugog [sic], Pendyrus, Morriston, Cwmbach and Manselton. This first record will lay the foundation for many more.

These were perceptive comments indeed. To close the year, an exciting invitation was accepted to participate in the London Welsh Association's St David's Day Festival at London's Royal Albert Hall in March 1964. Before that, however, there was to be the second in the series of annual concerts with Janet Coster and Ronald Lewis as guest artistes, both principals at the Royal Opera House, Covent Garden. All of this was a far cry from the Garnswllt Memorial Hall of barely two and a half years earlier.

By 1964 a routine of concerts had been established based on the principle of giving on average one a month. However, to this schedule would be added further radio and television broadcasts as well as competitions, all of which resulted in a particularly eventful diary for the young choristers. Some of the appearances brought their own prestige, contributing significantly to the choir's developing reputation, and the esteem in which it was now held. One such occasion was at Swansea's Brangwyn Hall on the evening of 25 January 1964 at a special rally of the Labour Party, then in opposition in the House of Commons. The previous day's *South Wales Evening Post* newspaper reported as follows:

> Tomorrow's attractions at the Brangwyn Hall, Swansea, are Mr Harold Wilson, Mr James Callaghan and the Pontarddulais Male Choir. The former two will, as you may well be aware, represent the Labour Party; the 125-strong singers of Pontarddulais admit to no such thing. Mr Noel Davies, 36-year-old schoolmaster who founded the choir three years ago, tells me that they have no political affiliation. They sing because they like singing and if anyone asks them they are glad to accept if they can… Tomorrow evening the choir, average age 30, will sing one piece in Welsh and one other song. More if there is time. They won't sing The Red Flag because 'we don't know it'.

There was a general election on the horizon, and Wilson was shortly to become Prime Minister with Callaghan as his Chancellor; Callaghan himself became Prime Minister over a decade later.

Côr Meibion Pontarddulais duly took its position on London's Albert Hall stage for the very first time on Saturday

7 March 1964 in the company of a host of other leading Welsh entertainers of the day. Ryan Davies was there, as were duettists 'Jac a Wil'; the guest accompanist was the renowned Welsh composer of memorable songs, Meirion Williams, and the community singing was led by a young Terry James. Highlights of the programme were broadcast on BBC radio the following Sunday evening, and the *Radio Times* succinctly summed up the significance of the annual festival for London Welshmen:

> Every Welshman has his own way of celebrating St David's Day. To the London Welshman it means anything from a homespun *noson lawen* in a suburban chapel to a grand occasion at the Savoy. But nearly everyone makes a point of being at the Royal Albert Hall for the festival organised by the London Welsh Association, for this is the one social get-together of the year where the Joneses who live in Croydon can be pretty sure of meeting the Williamses of Crouch End.

It was an occasion to remember as the first of many appearances at the unique venue, and an early example of the close links that were to be established over the years between the choir and numerous societies of Welsh exiles at home and abroad.

May was to be a busy month with major eisteddfod competitions, the choir gaining a second place at Pontrhydfendigaid and a first place a fortnight later at Cardigan. However, these were mere preludes to a breath-taking battle of the giants at the Swansea National in August. All of the 'big hitters' of the day were to appear in the 'Chief Male Voice' competition – Treorci, Morriston Orpheus, Manselton (later to become Swansea Male Choir), Pendyrus, Rhosllannerchrugog and Pontarddulais, all of whom had won the coveted first prize on previous occasions. On a sweltering afternoon at Singleton Park, when Glamorgan were famously defeating the touring Australian cricket team down the road at St Helens, thirty thousand people, some in the huge pavilion and others on the surrounding field, listened intently to the performances. The programme of set pieces was a challenging one in terms of its variety and complexity: a renaissance motet by Vittoria, 'Y Pren ar y Bryn' by the rapidly up and coming Welsh composer, William Mathias, and a musically demanding setting of Browning's poem 'Paracelsus' by the English composer Granville Bantock. The mammoth competition took well over two hours to complete, and the adjudication was awaited by all with that curious mix of apprehension and optimism. In a very closely fought contest the spoils went to the famous Treorci choir who were awarded a mere three marks more than second placed Pontarddulais. Treorci's well-known and much admired conductor, John Haydn Davies, had been whisked by car to the pavilion from his sick-bed, and promptly had to return there after his choir's performance, thus missing the result and the ensuing celebrations. On the one hand, Noel Davies and his choir were understandably disappointed, though on the other, they understood the significance of that memorable competition. In sporting parlance they were clearly in the first division, and they aimed to stay there.

The momentum generated over these first years was unstoppable, and in 1965 the choir embarked on an ambitious programme of a dozen concerts, six radio broadcasts and four competitive appearances, as well as the cutting of a second disc. No male choir had ever swept the board at all four of Wales's premier eisteddfodau within the same year. Now though, a precedent was set with victories at Pontrhydfendigaid, Cardigan, the Miners' Eisteddfod at Porthcawl as well as the National in Newtown, a remarkable feat in itself, but repeated by the Bont three years later.

And in addition to this whirlwind of activity, officers and committee were already finalising details and arrangements for the choir's first overseas visit. Complex issues of finance, insurance, travel and accommodation were addressed with vigour and energy, reflecting the rapidly developing expertise and confidence of the choir's administrative personnel.

Sweden was to host the choir's first foreign tour, with the invitation coming from the Tranas Male Choir via Olive Uhrfeldt, originally a native of Penllergaer, Swansea, and one of the Bont's most ardent supporters. She was to work closely with choir secretary Donald White through the process of building a tour itinerary that was to include visits to other Swedish male choirs in Växjö and Gislaved as well as Tranas itself. The secretary's powers of crisis management were tested to the full at the very last minute with the onset of an unexpected seamen's strike that necessitated the total reorganisation of the travel arrangements. As expected, he responded with the cheerful alacrity that the choir had come to expect from him, and the revised arrangements ran remarkably smoothly. Even for a community steeped in a rich choral tradition, this was a new experience, and the town's residents turned out in force on 26 May to wish the male choir well on its pioneering journey. In his *Chronicled History 1960–1972*, John Davies succinctly describes the busy schedule on tour:

> The highlights [at Tranas] included a visit to the famous glass-works and its displays at Kusta, the boat trip and picnic at Malexander, the reception and dinner at the Stadshotell and the concert at the High School prior to departure to Växjö. At this country town of Småland a visit to an open-air band concert, the concert at the concert-house and the never forgotten *smörgåsbord* were the highlights, and so to Gislaved, the smallest of the three centres visited prior to departure for native shores.

Two years later all three Swedish choirs returned to Pontarddulais for a reciprocal visit, and once again the townspeople turned out, this time for a rousing welcome parade. Some of the friendships forged lasted a lifetime and included that between Noel Davies and Ole Lindgren, conductor of the Tranas choir. Also well known in Sweden as a composer, Lindgren was to visit Wales on several occasions over coming years, attending various celebratory events as a guest of Côr Meibion Pontarddulais.

Seventeen other concerts were given during 1966 as well as numerous broadcasts. One of the BBC recordings provided further proof that the young choir had begun to forge an international reputation, as it appeared on the same programme as the Russian State Academy Choir, the Netherlands Chamber Choir and the Montreal Choral Society. A new venue was also added to the ever-increasing list of prestigious concert-halls at which the choir had performed – the impressively majestic Birmingham Town Hall. On the administrative side, there was to be a change of secretary in 1966, with Mansel Jenkins taking over from Donald White, and within a year Tom Coles had succeeded Gareth Davies, the choir's first and hitherto only chairman. At the same time, the financial reigns firmly held from the very beginning by Alun Rees, were handed over to John Davies, destined to become one of the choir's greatest servants over the decades to come.

For obvious reasons there had been no forays into competitive fields during 1966, but the healthy rivalry between the choirs of Pontarddulais and Treorci had continued to simmer quietly since the epic National Eisteddfod encounter of 1964. On returning to the eisteddfodic fold in 1967, though their illustrious opponents from the Rhondda Valley were not competing, Côr y Bont warmed up with yet another victory at Cardigan before embarking on their attempt to dethrone the mighty Treorci at the Bala National Eisteddfod. Once again the youngsters were to come off second best to their more experienced adversaries in another closely fought contest. News filtered through that this was to be Treorci's final eisteddfod appearance, as several of Wales's leading choirs at this time all abandoned the world of competition. Ostensibly this was in order to concentrate on concert work, recordings and overseas tours, though the cynic might have pointed to the fact that failure to do well in competition would do very little to enhance reputations in the increasingly lucrative market for recording contracts.

No one would have been particularly surprised had this disappointment led to a dent in morale in Pontarddulais. However, statistics from the registrar's report to that year's AGM showed that membership stood at a staggering 143, and that attendances for the month of October averaged almost 94 per cent. By this time the choir was preparing for its sixth annual concert, with the appearance of international stars Margaret Price and Stuart Burrows together with accompanist James Lockhart, emphasising again the choir's rapidly escalating reputation in being able to attract such celebrated guests. Significantly, the choir sang Schubert's eight-part choral masterpiece 'Song of the Spirits over the Waters' in this concert, another addition to an ever expanding repertoire, which not only included the staple traditional diet of male voice choirs, but also challenging music by classical composers as well as new, contemporary pieces. Thus from the early years, and consistently up until the present day, the choir's repertoire has remained a particularly eclectic one, reflecting a wide range of musical styles.

One casualty of the increasingly demanding schedule of the choir in 1968 was accompanist Elwyn Sweeting, who decided to retire from the post after six years of laudable service. His successor was a young sixth-form pupil at Gowerton Grammar School. Sixteen-year-old Wyn Davies was the son of local MP Ifor Davies, and his prodigious talent and musicality was evident from the outset, eliciting a sustained flow of commendations from distinguished critics and adjudicators. Pressures for the accompanist at concerts, broadcasts and competitions are formidable, especially so for such a young man, but Wyn carried out his duties confidently and with considerable authority and expertise over the next two years. His tenure, however, was to be comparatively brief as he went on to continue his musical studies at Christ Church College, Oxford, before eventually embarking upon an illustrious international career as a professional conductor and director of opera. Gowerton School's influence on the choir continued unabated as the teacher succeeded his pupil in the key post of accompanist. D Hugh Jones was head of the remarkable music department at the school, and stepped smoothly into his role at Pontarddulais, giving invaluable service as pianist and organist over the years to come. Another administrative change saw local schoolteacher Ifor Miles succeed Tom Coles as chairman in 1969.

As the choir approached its tenth anniversary it is well worth looking at the considerable repertoire established during that first decade of music making. Already described as eclectic, it reflected the view of the conductor that a concert programme should include something for everyone. Consequently there were arrangements of hymns and folk songs, spirituals, opera choruses, part songs as well as the traditional and popular Welsh male choir favourites such as 'Comrades in Arms', 'The Crusaders', 'Castilla', 'Martyrs of the Arena' and 'Nidaros'. There were works also from the mainstream classical tradition – motets from the renaissance period, often learned as eisteddfod test pieces; large scale choruses by composers such as Schubert, Grieg, Mendelssohn and Elgar; and there were challenging works by contemporary Welsh composers such as Mansel

Thomas, Arwel Hughes, William Mathias and Brian Hughes. Performances were also given of rarely heard works such as the 'Rhapsody for Contralto and Male Chorus' by Brahms. This wide-ranging repertoire, established from the earliest days, was to be a key feature of the choir's development over succeeding decades.

Arwel Hughes's music appeared in the demanding list of set pieces at the 'Chief' male choir competition at the Ammanford National Eisteddfod in 1970. His recently completed setting of 'Salm 148' was a 'test piece' in the true sense of the term. Added to this was another challenging work, 'Prospice', by D Vaughan Thomas, the distinguished musician who had contributed significantly to music making in Pontarddulais earlier in the century. The third piece, challenging in a different way, was yet another renaissance motet. It was a 'programme too far' for most male choirs, and, as we have seen, some of the more prestigious amongst them had by now turned their backs on the National Eisteddfod anyway. Côr Meibion Pontarddulais was the only entrant, and the victory something of a hollow one despite a stunning performance and the glowing praise of the adjudicators. During this celebratory year, there were also victories at the Cardigan and Porthcawl eisteddfodau, sixteen concerts, three television broadcasts, three radio broadcasts as well as a new LP record, *Glory in the Valley*. To mark the tenth birthday, and as a token of appreciation for their commitment and enthusiasm, all choir members were presented with a tie, specially designed for the celebration by chorister Tim Lewis, later to develop a reputation as a distinguished stained-glass artist. The musical highlight of the celebrations was to come towards the end of the year with the annual concert, an event tinged with a degree of controversy.

Despite attempts to improve and upgrade facilities at the Pontarddulais Welfare Hall, it was proving totally inadequate as a venue for high profile concerts. This presented Côr Meibion Pontarddulais with a dilemma, as it had become more and more obvious with each succeeding year that presenting the annual concert there was no longer a sustainable prospect. Yet, there was an understandable reluctance to relocate outside the immediate community, which had been so remarkably supportive over the choir's decade of existence. Ironically, there was no other venue within Pontarddulais itself that could offer suitable facilities. On the other hand, Swansea boasted one of the principality's grandest concert halls, with its comfortable seating for an audience of over a thousand, a substantial stage, a fine pipe organ and a stunning Steinway grand piano. The inevitable decision to relocate the choir's annual concert to the magnificent Brangwyn Hall did not please everyone at the time, though from 1970 onwards, it has been the venue without a single break in the series. Indeed, the event held usually towards the end of November is one of the established highlights of the Brangwyn's annual programme.

In true celebratory mood, the choir planned an ambitious concert in more ways than one, with innovation as an obvious theme. The venue was new and so was the format of the concert's printed programme. Gone were the flimsy sheets of the past, which had done little more than outline what music was to be performed. The new style brochure went considerably further, with biographical details of the participants, lists of supporting patrons, and advertisements and messages of greetings on the choir's tenth birthday. Four highly respected singers were engaged as guest artistes – Rae Woodland, soprano (standing in for the indisposed Elizabeth Vaughan); Jean Allister, contralto; Stuart Burrows, tenor; and Delme Bryn Jones, bass. All were accompanied by guest accompanist Richard Nunn, and Wyn Davies also returned as a guest to accompany the choir. Distinguished guests and local dignitaries had been invited and there was a great sense of occasion.

Challenging contemporary music had been a feature of the choir's repertoire since the earliest days, but now, as another innovation for the celebratory concert, they commissioned a new piece for the first time. Already familiar with his music, the musical director approached none other than William Mathias, a Welsh composer of international stature. His ready and enthusiastic acceptance of the commission was a clear indication of the considerable respect in which the choir was now held. Conscious of the concert venue, Mathias decided on a setting of the 'Gloria' for male choir and organ. He knew of the unusual trumpet stop on the Brangwyn Hall organ, and much of the accompaniment adopts a fanfare style, whereas the choir has to respond to complex syncopated rhythms, long-held chords and occasional writing for eight vocal parts. It could fairly be described as a virtuoso piece in all respects, and Mathias, present for the first performance, was delighted, acknowledging the superb performance and the prowess of choir, organist and conductor.

Concerns originally expressed by some at the decision to hold the event in Swansea had been dissipated to a great degree through the provision of a fleet of subsidised buses ferrying concertgoers to and from the Brangwyn Hall. The undoubted musical success together with the splendour of the venue convinced the few remaining doubters that the decision had indeed been a wise one.

At the very first concert in the Garnswllt Village Hall a decade earlier, as the fledgling choir was only just beginning to find its feet, who could have anticipated the remarkable success story that was to follow? And, where next for Côr Meibion Pontarddulais? In the Annual General Meeting held towards the end of 1970, the musical director kept his message simple. Paraphrasing the title of a newly learned piece by Grieg, he underlined the obvious and said, 'Brothers, sing on!'

2

CONSOLIDATION (1971–85)

'BROTHERS, SING ON!' AND that is exactly what the choir did. The routine had been established. There were concerts at home and away in 1971, including the reaffirmation of strengthening associations with Welsh societies in Chelmsford and Birmingham; requests for radio and television recordings continued to pour in; and there were further eisteddfod successes too. But the ultimate challenge was how to follow the previous year's remarkable annual concert. As always, Noel Davies had planned ahead and knew exactly what he wanted to do. He had developed a special friendship with the legendary conductor of the Treorci Male Choir, so often the adversaries on the eisteddfod platform. Not surprisingly, John Haydn Davies and Noel Davies had developed a special rapport, undoubtedly derived from similar social backgrounds and strong Christian principles. Noel, having already tackled several choruses of the *Requiem* by Luigi Cherubini with his choir, was encouraged by John Haydn to prepare and perform the complete work. Such extended settings for male choir are very rare in the repertoire, and all seven sections are set for chorus with no solos whatsoever. The entire mass was committed to memory in Latin and performed with a local orchestra at the 1971 annual concert. It was another *tour de force*. Over the years to come the choir performed Cherubini's *Requiem in D minor* on several other occasions, including in the Cardiff Choral Festival in 1978 with the Philharmonia Orchestra under the direction of George Guest, a performance broadcast by HTV, and again in the choir's twenty-fifth anniversary concert in 1985 with the Welsh Sinfonia Orchestra.

The now firmly established routine of concerts, broadcasts and competitions continued unabated in 1972. Away visits were on the increase, and concerts were given for Harlow's Welsh Society, as part of Bath Silver Ring Choir's anniversary celebrations and at a cider festival in Hereford. A fifth 'National' win was secured at Haverfordwest where the Mathias 'Gloria', the choir's very own commission, was one of the test pieces. The diverse nature of the choir's music making was reflected in invitations to join significant figures from the world of light entertainment in UK- wide television broadcasts, such as the *Sounds of Secombe* programme broadcast as part of the BBC's fiftieth anniversary celebrations.

Amidst the now regular and accepted round of rehearsals and performances, correspondence was received from half way across the world, which was to prove a springboard for exciting developments over the coming years. In a committee meeting held on 30 January 1972, the following was minuted:

> The Secretary noted that a Canadian School Choir required accommodation in the area for the period 30th March–6th April 1972. A possible exchange visit could be forthcoming in 1973 to Montreal. It was unanimously agreed that we invite the choir to Pontarddulais on the dates mentioned, the Secretary to arrange preliminary details by telephone.

Former treasurer, John Davies, was now secretary, and financial matters had been handed over to founder member Alun Davies, another who was to become one of the choir's great servants over the decades to come. With Ifor Miles continuing as chairman, this was the enthusiastic trio entrusted with the considerable administrative challenges that lay ahead. But who was behind the Canadian request, and why was it directed at the Pontarddulais Male Choir?

The connection lay in the Pontarddulais Youth Club of the 1950s, which had of course spawned the male choir itself. One of the club's members had been Iwan Edwards who, having qualified as a music teacher, had emigrated to Canada and become Head of Music at a high school in Lachine, a suburb of Montreal. In a hurriedly organised trip, he was bringing his school choir and wind band to Wales. Anxious to renew his links with Pontarddulais, he had already formulated a plan that this should be the first leg of an exchange visit. The young people were welcomed warmly during the first week of April, and their brief visit was packed with receptions, day trips, presentations and a concert at the Welfare Hall, and another at Tregaron. Significantly, within three weeks of their departure, the following minute was recorded in a meeting of the male choir's committee:

An estimate of the airfare was quoted at £60 (ex Cardiff to Montreal) per person. The tour would be for a duration of a maximum of 10 days in Canada with three concerts.

Thus planning for the return visit had commenced swiftly, with due regard to the considerable costs involved and the need for a purposeful fund-raising drive to begin without delay. The prowess of the Pontarddulais Male Choir in being able to attract world-class singers to join them on the concert platform was reflected in a brief minute at the same committee meeting, which simply mentioned with regards the next annual concert, the 'confirmation of Miss Te Kanawa's availability'.

An initial target of £9,000 was set for a Canadian tour fund, half of which had been accumulated by March 1973. Although a variety of fund raising initiatives and events had been devised, the primary source of income was to be the choir's weekly tote. The usual round of concerts for worthwhile charities and organisations were now supplemented by the choir's own concerts with a view to amplifying tour funds, and one of the highlights in this context was a concert given by great rivals and friends, Côr Meibion Treorci, to a packed Ebenezer Chapel in Gorseinon. Treorci was not the only world-renowned male choir to link up with the Bont at this time, and through the auspices of Noel Davies's great friend from the days of Coleg Harlech, Meredydd Evans, by then with the BBC, the famous Harvard Glee Club gave a concert at the Pontarddulais Welfare Hall in mid August.

Administrative and musical challenges had to be faced if the ambitious Canadian tour was to prove a success, with many complex issues being addressed with vigour. Transportation including flights, insurance, concert programmes, general itineraries, accommodation, gifts for presentations and a host of other matters were dealt with expediently and professionally by a small but dedicated committee, inspirationally led by the trio of officers mentioned above. With a musical reputation of considerable distinction to uphold, any general lapses in discipline within choir ranks, which threatened to undermine standards, were simply not tolerated. Members whose attendance at rehearsals and concerts were deemed to be unsatisfactory were not allowed on tour, and occasionally a chorister was required to leave the choir permanently.

Local baritone Nigel Hopkins was invited to join the choir on tour as a soloist, but a late blow was suffered when choir accompanist D Hugh Jones was forced to withdraw through illness. As a Bont youngster, I had worked briefly as accompanist with Noel at the youth club in the 1960s, and whilst at college had helped out with the male choir in emergencies at occasional rehearsals and concerts. I joined the choir on tour, and though never formally appointed, remained as the accompanist for the next eighteen years. Final arrangements were in place, with a departure from Gatwick Airport with Laker Airways on 29 September, returning from Toronto on 13 October, with 98 travelling, including conductor, accompanist and soloist.

In his booklet, *Chronicled History 1960–1972*, written as part of the preparations for the Canadian visit, John Davies acknowledges the preparatory work undertaken by key personnel in the centres where concerts were to be held. Terry Pearce and Iwan Edwards in Montreal, Don Mills in Ottawa and Malcolm Williams in Kingston had indeed all worked tirelessly. In all respects, the tour was a tremendous success, with the music-making actually commencing on the giant DC10 aircraft as the choir entertained fellow passengers on the outward journey. The choir's important links with Welsh Societies in the United Kingdom were now extended to Canada, and welcoming hosts at Kingston and Ottawa were enthusiastic members of the respective Welsh Societies there. The concert at Kingston took place in the impressive Grant Hall of Queen's University, and formed a part of the town's tercentenary celebrations. The choir's arrival at Lachine meant the renewal of friendships formed a year earlier with the youngsters of the high school during their visit to Wales, and an opportunity of meeting their parents who hosted the choristers. As well as a concert at the high school itself, a second was given at Salle Claude Champagne, the music school of the University of Montreal. The final concert of the tour took place at the magnificent Ottawa Arts Centre in the presence of the Governor General of Canada and a capacity audience of 2,500 people. All performances on tour were greeted with tumultuous standing ovations, and the remainder of a busy schedule was littered with television and radio broadcasts, informal musical gatherings and official receptions and presentations.

Not surprisingly, the Pontarddulais choristers had helped

re-invigorate a sense of community spirit in those centres visited, with many immigrants palpably and emotionally reminded of their Welsh roots, so much so that plans were afoot almost immediately to organise a second tour to eastern Canada. Experience had shown that this would be a long term project, as the choir on its return once more embarked on its busy schedule on home soil.

To complicate matters, concert-engagements were now being accepted so far ahead that the choir diary was already virtually full for the next three years – a trend that was set to continue. Apart from the pleas for a return visit to Canada, requests came to consider tours to Hungary, USA, New Zealand and Germany sometime in the future. Administratively, there were time-consuming enquiries and plans to be made, and this with a new chairman in place – the affable and genial schoolmaster Hugh Morgan, who was to lead wisely over the coming years. What better way to guard against anticlimax following the Canadian tour than to re-energize with two major competitions in 1974. The unbeaten tag continued, with famous victories at Cardigan and at the Bro Myrddin National Eisteddfod in Carmarthen.

It is worth dwelling for a moment on the programme of music selected for the 1974 annual concert. The second half was a feast of 'lollipops', but the opening half was an unprecedented extravaganza of classical pieces accompanied by the City of Swansea Orchestra. Rarely, if ever, had a male choir attempted such an ambitious programme of infrequently heard works, which read as follows:

'O Praise the Lord with one Consent' (Chandos Anthem)	Handel
'The Last Words of David'	Randall Thompson
'Alto Rhapsody' (with soloist, Elizabeth Bainbridge)	Brahms
'Song of the Spirits over the Waters'	Schubert
'Songs of the Sea' (with soloist, Eric Shilling)	Stanford

Detailed programme notes on each piece were provided for the audience, and as if the first half of music hadn't sufficiently taxed the stamina of the singers, the concert ended with Protheroe's 'Nidaros'. The evening was tinged with nostalgia, as the leader of the orchestra, the jovial and irrepressible Morgan Lloyd took his final bow before retirement.

Another appearance at London's Royal Albert Hall added further spice to what had been a remarkable year. Noel Davies however, with feet as always firmly on the ground, warned against complacency. In his speech at the Annual General Meeting towards the end of the year, he mused, 'I look forward to another satisfying year in 1975 provided we do not fall into the pitfall of being over-confident'.

As well as two television broadcasts and cutting a new long playing record, the fifteen concerts of 1975 included performances at the Fife Arts Festival in St Andrews and for the Birmingham Welsh Society once again at the splendid Town Hall. In recognition of its commitment to competing regularly at the National Eisteddfod, the choir was invited to participate in one of the festival's evening concerts in Cricieth, a 'National' appearance that was thankfully not accompanied by the usual stresses, strains and nerves inevitably associated with the competitive arena. And so to the Annual General Meeting towards the end of 1975, when reference was made to the dissatisfaction of choristers with the regular bus contractors, whose coaches, amongst other things, were deemed to be rather on the slow side. Indeed, such was the concern that the poor company forfeited the contract, with chairman Hugh Morgan explaining, 'The straw that broke the camel's back came when Morriston Orpheus flew past us in Eynon's coaches during our return trip from Scotland earlier this year'. Some things obviously touched a raw nerve! At the same AGM, Noel Davies noted that a sure sign that the choir had 'arrived' was that people asked for 'anything by the Bont' on radio request programmes. More importantly, he had, as always, a thought-provoking message for his choristers, on this occasion through quoting the words of Harry Secombe:

> It's easy to rest on your laurels when you get near the top of this game. But that's the way to grow old quickly. If I don't keep pushing myself, those laurels will turn into a wreath – there's nothing surer than that!

Perhaps the least said the better about 1976, which became infamously known as 'the year of the protest'. It was a long time ago, and those involved, no doubt older and wiser, now look back with wry smiles on their faces. Having been declared winners yet again at the National Eisteddfod, on this occasion in Cardigan, the Bont faced an official protest from a rival choir on the grounds that one of the adjudicating panel had worked professionally with the victors. 'Cythraul y canu' was alive and kicking! The story is worth retelling for two reasons. First of all, the protest and its subsequent immediate dismissal by Eisteddfod authorities was met with a dignified silence from the Bont. Secondly, however, Noel Davies felt that a musical riposte was in order. There had been no intention that year of competing at the Miners' Eisteddfod in Porthcawl, but as the choir reconvened following the summer recess, the conductor announced that they would be going after all. It was only a coincidence that their rivals at the Cardigan National were also competing in Porthcawl. The point was made with another victory, and this time there were hearty congratulations all round.

Arrangements had proceeded with zeal and alacrity in preparation for the second Canadian tour, now finalised to take place towards the end of May and beginning of June 1977. Administratively, several key officers were able to draw on their considerable experience from the previous tour in terms of securing the necessary funding and organising the travel arrangements. Musically, the choir took with it the eclectic mix of pieces that had formed the basis of its repertoire from the very beginning. Audiences at home and abroad were required to tune in to arrangements of 'pop' music one minute, and to readjust the next by listening to music by classical composers and complex contemporary pieces. It was an unusual pot-pourri of music, which nevertheless had its own attractive appeal, derived from the conductor's mantra that a concert programme should include something to suit everyone's taste. Pieces within the repertoire came and went to a certain degree of course, and often returned after a long absence, but it is sobering to note that since the choir's foundation up until the second Canadian tour of 1977 almost two hundred individual pieces of music had been learnt, in a variety of languages, all of which had been committed to memory.

Hosts for this second Canadian visit were the Welsh Societies of Ottawa and Kingston, the Deep River Rugby Club, the Montreal Welsh Male Voice Choir, and of course the Lachine High School. Despite a hectic schedule of concerts, receptions and informal social events, everything ran smoothly and efficiently, and the Canadian press was warm in its praise and enthusiasm. Notwithstanding the many references to the musical quality of the choir's performances in the press generally, it is particularly interesting to quote from a passage that appeared in the *Whig-Standard* on 4 June. After all, the Quebec area of Canada had its own bilingual dimension, and the comments are particularly incisive in terms of analysing what it can mean for a smaller cultural entity existing side by side with one of the world's most powerful linguistic influences. Ironically of course, French was the great linguistic power in the eyes of the English-speaking minority within Quebec. Of the choir's performances the newspaper critic wrote:

There is a certain intensity of expression that belongs to communities which have had to accommodate one side of their lives to the language and to some extent to the modes of thought of an alien race. In Canada we are beginning to understand something of that, and perhaps it was this factor that made the singing of 'O Canada' at the beginning of this concert, and 'Mae Hen Wlad fy Nhadau' at the end of it so moving.

Upshots of that second Canadian tour included the welcoming of Jeannette Hudson, tour organiser in Canada, to Pontarddulais in October, and a rather hectic five-day visit of the Ottawa Welsh Society Choir during August 1978. In appreciation and recognition of his charismatic personality and musical prowess Noel Davies was invited to conduct the 1978 North American Cymanfa Ganu, sponsored by the Ottawa Welsh Society, a festival acclaimed as one of the best ever. Such was the rapport established between the choir and its Canadian friends that within two years an invitation had been received to undertake a third tour of eastern Canada.

Since 1968, and the National Eisteddfod at Barry, the choir had established a pattern of competing at the 'National' in the south. Consequently, attention turned to the Festival to be held at Cardiff in 1978, and in terms of test pieces, the choir was faced with the most challenging of programmes. William Mathias's musical idiom was already familiar, though his 'Nos a Bore' was new to the choir. This beautifully evocative setting describes a late night storm in the Menai straights, followed by the peace and tranquillity of the following morning when memories of the storm have all but faded. The obvious challenge here was to convey extremes of dynamics within a comparatively short piece. Zoltan Kodaly's unaccompanied part song 'The Peacocks' demanded disciplined singing, and 'The Dream of Llewelyn ap Gruffydd', by the Englishman Alan Bush, was a monumental test of stamina and control. Technical difficulties were faced and overcome through sheer hard work, diligence and determination. It has to be said that this was a contemporary programme beyond most Welsh male choirs of the day, but the Pontarddulais performances drew particularly complimentary comments from the adjudicating panel, and the eighth 'National' win was secured.

Consideration of the accumulating requests for further overseas tours mentioned earlier had continued, though the considerable degree of research and planning had virtually come to nothing, primarily because of financial constraints. However, this was to change following a visit to one of the choir's rehearsals by Gwyndaf Jones, who had been the choir's very first vice chairman, and indeed the only deputy conductor ever appointed. Gwyndaf by this time was a civilian schoolmaster on an RAF base in Wildenrath, Germany, and his proposal that the choir should visit and perform there was greeted with warm approval. A key change in administrative personnel had seen John Gronow take over from John Davies as secretary following the Canadian visit, and it was on his shoulders that much of the responsibility now fell in preparation for the visit to Germany. Once again the choir was fortunate in yet another fine servant, whose considerable administrative skills had been refined during his period as assistant secretary over preceding years.

A long journey to Dover, a ferry crossing to Zeebrugge and a further coach journey from the Belgian port saw the choir arrive at Wildenrath in the middle of a particularly bitter snap of arctic weather in January 1979. In recent years, the choir's president had been concerned, because of his increasingly onerous duties at the University in Swansea, that he was unable to devote time to his responsibilities with regards the choir. Indeed choir officials had to move quickly to persuade him from resigning. Happily, by the time of the Wildenrath visit, he was able to join the choir, for the first time on an overseas visit, and thoroughly enjoyed the experience, and his relationship with the choir was reaffirmed to everyone's delight. Two concerts were to be given, the first at the church on the RAF base, and the second at nearby JHQ Rheindahlen. Musically and socially, this 'tour' was again a resounding success, though with one incident that could have led to chaos.

After the choir had departed the RAF base and had arrived safely for the concert at Rheindahlen, the atrocious weather deteriorated significantly with increasingly freezing conditions. Guest artistes, Pontarddulais's very own Patricia and Dennis O'Neill, had also managed to reach the concert hall at Rheindahlen before the weather closed in. Back in Wildenrath however, the Commanding Officer, John Mitchell, had closed the base, with no-one allowed to leave because of treacherous and dangerous road conditions outside. Choir and guest artistes were already at Rheindahlen with a capacity audience waiting in anticipation. But, and rather an important 'but' under the circumstances, both musical director and accompanist were stranded at Wildenrath. High level discussions rather hastily took place and Mitchell, realising the potential catastrophe, allowed one staff car, and one only, to leave the base with Noel Davies and Eric Jones aboard. The concert, scheduled to start at 8.00 pm, actually started at 10.00 pm and concluded, to rapturous applause well after midnight.

Pressures from Canada continued for a third visit, but with estimates of costs beyond £27,000, arrangements were put on hold. A celebration of the tenth anniversary of the Investiture of the Prince of Wales resulted in a prestigious invitation for Wales's premier male choir to perform at Caernarfon Castle in a special concert broadcast on network television. Hugh Morgan vacated the Chair to Edward Morgan at the end of 1979, and at that year's Annual General Meeting, in his address, Noel Davies quoted Longfellow:

Lives of great men all remind us
We can make our lives sublime;
And, departing leave behind us
Footprints on the sands of time.

Within six months of the visit to Germany, an invitation was received to revisit Rheindahlen. Choir officials hesitated, and rightfully so, because another request was shortly received from Wildenrath, with plans this time to perform in local German communities outside the RAF bases. Huckelhoven and Kleingladbach had their own male choirs, and were communities with a strong mining tradition not unlike that of Pontarddulais. On this occasion as guest artistes, Patricia O'Neill, once more invited to link up with the choir on a second German visit, was joined by schoolmaster and fine baritone John Davies, another Bont boy, who had been a member of Noel Davies's youth choir back in the 1950s. The weather on this occasion in May 1980 presented no problems, and John Mitchell's successor as Commanding Officer, Danny Lavender, was equally as cordial in his warm welcome, and the concert at Rheindahlen was given in the presence of Air Marshall Sir Peter Terry, Commander in Chief, RAF Germany. It was a time when the Cold War was at its height, and during the choir's stay at Wildenrath the base actually experienced a 'red alert' when Phantom jets were hurriedly scrambled in order to confront interloping Soviet planes.

There was to be no competing for the choir on their doorstep at the Dyffryn Lliw National Eisteddfod held at Gowerton in 1980. This was due to the involvement of conductor and accompanist in various eisteddfod committees, which precluded their participation in competitions. Yet it was still to be a busy week for the choir, with an appearance at the opening evening concert, and later in the week in combination with the West Glamorgan Youth

Choir in an electrifying performance of Carl Orff's stunning *Carmina Burana*. Noel Davies conducted the festival's closing Cymanfa Ganu.

Suddenly, or seemingly so, the twenty-first anniversary was on the horizon, and once again the choir turned to the experienced John Davies to co-ordinate the celebrations. The usual busy round of concerts in 1981 was now richly supplemented by several social occasions of a celebratory nature. Chief guest at a May dinner dance was the Commanding Officer at Wildenrath during the choir's first visit, now Air-Commodore John Mitchell. A month later, once again the great rivals of the Bont in the 1960s, and subsequently their greatest of friends, Treorci Male Choir came to join in the special birthday, with an outstanding display of male choral singing at Gorseinon's Ebenezer Chapel. The Treorci connection continued with the formal anniversary dinner at Swansea's Dragon hotel in October when emeritus conductor John Haydn Davies proposed the toast to Noel Davies and the Pontarddulais Male Choir. Chief guest was Cliff Morgan, then Head of Outside Broadcasts with BBC Television.

For various reasons, the choir had not competed at the 'National' since 1978. What better time to re-enter the fray than in the 'coming of age' year? Another victory was secured at Machynlleth, and the record-breaking series was extended yet again. At the same eisteddfod Noel Davies was installed as an honorary member of the Gorsedd, as an acknowledgement of his remarkable contribution to the tradition of male choral music in Wales. Reconvening after the traditional summer recess, priority was given to preparations for the twenty-first anniversary concert at the Brangwyn Hall.

This was to be a grand affair with four guest artistes, all having special connections with the choir. It was a night to remember with memorable musical contributions from

Janet Price, Doreen O'Neill, Stuart Burrows and Delme Bryn Jones. Bridging the first and latest of the 'annual concerts' the choir's programme included Daniel Protheroe's 'Crusaders', which they had sung at the equivalent event in 1962 at the Pontarddulais Welfare Hall, and a new commission from the choir's accompanist, Eric Jones, a setting of Waldo Williams's 'Rhodia Wynt'.

Visits to far flung corners of England, and Scotland too, had become increasingly frequent as the years went by, with challenging consequences particularly regarding costs. On booking the services of the choir, concert organisers were asked only to contribute travelling expenses. Yet logically, an overnight stay would be the sensible option when considering a coach journey home of four hours or more. So often, the charitable organisations arranging the concerts could ill afford to pay for overnight accommodation for a hundred or more choristers. Paying from the choir's own reserves would have adversely affected the on-going drive to ensure sufficient funds for overseas tours. Occasionally, particularly when concerts were organised by Welsh Societies in the larger English towns and cities, choir members were accommodated in private homes, but more often than not, they faced a long trek home instead. Invariably, as a mark of appreciation for the choir's performance, the concert would be followed by a reception, which almost always developed into a convivial, informal singsong. Even if officers succeeded in getting choristers to the buses by midnight, it was by no means unusual to be arriving home at the break of dawn. Yet, how could this choir refuse invitations to prestigious events that others could only dream of receiving in the first place? Thus in 1982 the choir included in its concert schedule performances at Chichester Cathedral and the Perth Festival of Arts in Scotland.

Most choir members by this time had increasing parental responsibilities as family men, and a large number were still shift workers at the local mines and tinplate works. Others had assumed managerial posts of considerable commitment in various professional spheres. Juggling home life, work schedules and the formidable time demands emanating from conscientious membership of Côr Meibion Pontarddulais was by no means an easy task. Some stalwarts left the choir, many though to return to the fold years later, when children had grown up or when retirement had arrived. The continuing influx of new members still kept overall figures buoyant and membership rarely dipped below 115.

Two other highlights of 1982 were a tenth victory at the 'National', on this occasion 'down the road' at Swansea's Singleton Park, and a performance on the newly established Welsh-language television channel, S4C. There was to be a third highlight for the choir's musical director, and one that reflected the considerable esteem in which he was held in the male choral singing world. He took charge of the 1,000 male voices concert at the Royal Albert Hall, to such acclaim that he was accorded a rare second invitation two years later. The appearance at the National Eisteddfod was to be the choir's last for twelve years. They had been regular competitors since their first appearance in 1962, acknowledging the eisteddfod's significant role historically in fostering and nurturing choral music in Wales. That conviction remained, the reason for the choir's absence over coming years being that Noel Davies, and his accompanist also, were receiving invitations to adjudicate at the National Eisteddfod.

References have already been made to the choir's liberal approach towards the different styles of music assimilated into the repertoire; the eclectic mix of music tackled over the years; and the attitude of 'something for everyone' in concert programmes. But who would have coupled the names of Pink Floyd and Côr Meibion Pontarddulais? As if 1982 did not already have its wide range of challenges, a brand new and very different one awaited the choir. Some three years earlier the iconic rock group had released their startling album, *The Wall*, to international acclaim. Roger Waters, one of the group's founders, felt that the original project, which involved a psychologically complex story of a disillusioned rock star, could be developed into a cinematic film. He was keen to energise and emotionally enhance the original recording tracks and was particularly interested in using men's voices, although by his own admission was unsure of exactly how to do so. He wanted to experiment; he wanted to work with singers who could be musically flexible; he wanted to explore in an improvisatory way with experienced musicians. He decided to work with Côr Meibion Pontarddulais.

It turned out to be the strangest of recording sessions, as he and his entourage set up a complex array of microphones in the usual rehearsal venue of the primary school hall, all linked to a mobile studio of unbelievable technical wizardry parked outside on the school yard. Different vocal combinations were tried, chords were revised and rearranged, musical lines were continually readjusted, and the recorded results taken away for mixing. The outcome was a richly intense and expressively absorbing sound track. Waters was not to forget his successful liaison with Côr y Bont, as testified by his reappearance with a second project on his mind several years later.

Officers and committee continued to juggle various enquiries regarding foreign tours, researching and debating what could and could not be undertaken realistically. Czechoslovakia was added to the list towards the beginning of 1983, as was Portugal, and it was the latter that was to claim a sharp focus of attention, as a realisation dawned that such a visit could prove a viable proposition logistically, financially and musically. Long term planning commenced.

Another recognition of the choir's standing came in the

form of a prestigious invitation to perform at the opening concert of the newly completed St David's Hall in Cardiff in the presence of HRH The Queen Mother and broadcast live on network television. This was one of twenty engagements during 1983, including the choir's fifth appearance at the Royal Albert Hall, and it was a year that also saw the cutting of yet another LP record. This again was a time of particularly interesting additions to the repertoire, inevitably emphasising a wide range of musical styles. In rehearsals the choir would move seamlessly from perfecting Max Bruch's Psalm 23 to working on Welsh contemporary composer Brian Hughes's piece, 'Bywyd y Bugail', to polishing the final touches of spirituals such as 'I got shoes' and 'Ride the Chariot'.

At a committee meeting held in May 1984 the choir's experienced treasurer, Alun Davies, noted with delight that choir funds were in excess of £20,000 for the first time in its history. This augured well for the Portugal plan, which was however to stall slightly as renewed pressures for tours came at this time from previously visited Canada and Sweden, as well as from California. Ironically, at the same time, the mining fraternity within the choir were falling into arrears with their tote payments, a sure sign of the social consequences of pit closures and the miners' strike. As the miners' dispute intensified, there were concerns that the conflict could resonate within the choir's ranks. After all, represented within the membership were union activists, flying pickets, management and police. The bonds formed through singing together overcame any potential difficulties, and there were no problems.

On the threshold of the twenty-fifth anniversary year, John Davies commenced a second term of onerous duties as secretary, and president Ieuan Williams was busy compiling a history of the choir in readiness for the quarter centenary celebrations. Looking back, he analyses the basis of the choir's undoubted success, emphasising routine procedures as well as more complex administrative challenges, whilst never forgetting the central *raison d'être* of musical excellence. It is worth briefly quoting from his eloquent discourse, for the principles still apply:

> ...closely knit internal structures can also be seen at work helping to resolve problems of a more routine kind that multiplied and became more sophisticated over the years; problems associated with issues having legal implications such as insurance, taxation and charitable status; with the complex resolution of individual and corporate responsibility in relation to matters seemingly as different as the provision of a uniform dress and the formulating of a satisfactory constitution. They have played an important part also in initiating, assessing and applying sensibly new ideas having to do for instance with social activities of many kinds, with publicity and with providing information for members, especially new members. Most important of all perhaps, these close internal ties have served the Choir particularly well in the consistent pursuit of basic broadly based principles – the quality of singing and its close relationship with the discipline of good order and conduct as well as with musicianship; the maintenance of cordial relations within and outside the Choir; service to deserving causes within the Choir itself, in the local community and especially in society at large.

Whether by design or accident, a quarter century of music making was celebrated with many opportunities of looking back to past achievements, of linking up once more with musical friends and associates, and of revisiting concert venues that had been of particular significance in the history of the choir. February saw the choir join forces once again with Dennis O'Neill at a glittering charity concert at Cardiff's

St David's Hall in the presence of HRH Diana Princess of Wales. In the few intervening years since the first Wildenrath visit, the international reputation of the Pontarddulais born tenor had burgeoned remarkably, and by this time he had already established himself as an outstanding singer on the world's operatic stage. The prestigious event at Cardiff had as its patron Sir Geraint Evans, another of the choir's oldest and dearest friends.

Links with overseas agencies were recalled with concerts for RAF Credenhall in Hereford Cathedral, and there was to be a reaffirmation also of important connections with several charities supported by the choir over the years. This included another concert for leukaemia research, given under the auspices of the Canton Cardiff Citadel. Ironically, and sadly, there was no chapel in Pontarddulais that could accommodate a large choir on a front gallery, and so it was that Gorseinon's Ebenezer Chapel had become the choir's spiritual home from home, and a concert was also given there during this special celebratory year.

Chief guest at the anniversary dinner-dance in October was the revered English musician Dr George Guest. English, because of his long association with St John's College, Cambridge and its splendid world-renowned choir. But Welsh also, through his ancestry and his remarkable achievement of learning the Welsh language as an adult. I recall working with him as an adjudicator at the National Eisteddfod, and such was his professionalism and commitment to getting things absolutely right, that he would ask his fellow adjudicators to 'look over' his Welsh before he delivered the adjudication from the stage. There was no need. George Guest had formed a close relationship with the choir, and had adjudicated them and conducted them on several occasions. He was the ideal choice as guest of honour.

Noel Davies could have gone for an array of international stars to join the choir at its twenty-fifth anniversary annual concert at Swansea's Brangwyn Hall. In his own innovative style, however, he decided to keep the vocal contribution firmly in the hands, or rather voices, of his beloved choir. With an orchestra assembled for the special evening, supporting artistes were to be instrumentalists, most of whom had direct association with the town of Pontarddulais. Haldon Evans and Michael Downing (trumpets), David Thomas (violin) and Eric Jones (piano) were all Pontarddulais born and bred. The exception was another very good friend of very long standing, organist Huw Tregelles Williams. Another first half performance of Cherubini's *Requiem* was complemented with a second half blend of concerto movements and classical choral pieces, a combination that fired the capacity audience with considerable enthusiasm. With all of this formidable celebratory activity going on, it was all the more remarkable that the choir found the time to record another LP.

It had been a time therefore of looking back, rightly enjoying the opportunity of reflecting on past achievements. However, as acknowledged by the choir and musical team at the helm, this in itself would be futile unless such successes were replicated, new challenges met and new peaks scaled.

What had become of the requests for overseas tours, which the choir officials had been carefully appraising? One project was forcing itself to the fore, and a substantial amount of time during the celebrations of 1985 was quietly, but enthusiastically spent by officials in planning a tour to Portugal. What better way to commence the second quarter of a century?

3

CONTINUING SUCCESSES (1986–2002)

ARRANGEMENTS FOR THE VISIT to Portugal had continued purposefully throughout the twenty-fifth anniversary year, and at the beginning of 1986 the choir's focus was clearly on this new venture due to take place in February. However, there was a special diversion of attention at the announcement of the New Year's Honours List, which included the name of Noel Davies, the choir's inspirational and charismatic founder conductor. Rarely could the awarding of an MBE have been greeted and celebrated with more genuine enthusiasm and joy than this particular one, and how appropriate that it came in recognition of a quarter of a century of visionary leadership and unbounded enthusiasm. With typical humility, the great man himself deflected all praise and messages of congratulations towards his choir, claiming that the recognition was down to the dedication and hard work of his choristers.

By a happy coincidence, another name appearing on the same list of recipients was that of Jack Clift, a great admirer of the choir and one of the stalwarts of the Warwickshire Friends of Home Farm Trust. The trust had links with similar agencies in Portugal, and it was Jack Clift who had worked tirelessly to develop those links, which enabled the choir's visit to take place. From the beginning, the musical objectives of the tour were to be complemented by ones of a philanthropic and benevolent nature. Jack Clift worked closely with Pat Potier who had been keenly involved in fund raising for Portugal's disabled young people through the auspices of the country's *Liga Portugesa Dos Deficientes Motores*. Initially, Pat Potier mentioned the project to Robin Jowit of Robbialac Portuguesa, who in turn commenced discussions with some of his extensive business contacts in Portugal. This resulted in a remarkable package of sponsorship for the tour by influential British companies, which led to the formation of *Amigos Britanicos de Portugal*, whose deliberations were skilfully chaired by d'Arcy Orders. All six of those companies had important links with Portugal, or significant bases within the country itself. British Petroleum, Commercial Union Assurance, Imperial Chemical Industries, Lloyd's Bank International, Reckitt and Robbialac all combined forces with Anglo Portuguese News, British Airways and the British Council, to constitute a formidable partnership offering support and patronage. Substantial funds were raised for much needed equipment and resources for the young people, and equally importantly, the profile of agencies working with the disabled youngsters was raised significantly.

The opening concert of the tour was given at Lisbon's Teatro Nacional de São Carlos, before the choir travelled north to the university town of Coimbra, where they performed at the Teatro Academico de Gil Vincente. Returning to the capital, the final concert was at the Teatro Municipal de São Luiz. The choir's performances were beautifully complemented by the virtuoso playing of the young Welsh harpist, Caryl Thomas.

Once again at this time, the choir received several enquiries regarding the possibility of further overseas tours, including a return to Portugal. Danny Lavender, Commanding Officer during the choir's second visit to

Wildenrath was now keen to see the choir visit Norway, and over succeeding years invitations came from Belgium and again from Sweden, where Noel Davies's old friend, Ole Lindgren, wished to replicate the choir's tour there of 1966. Such undertakings for a large body of amateur choristers, most of whom also had working and family commitments, had to be considered carefully, not to mention the obvious financial challenges also involved in raising sufficient funds and securing sponsorship. There were to be no immediate foreign visits, but 1987 saw the choir enjoy very different and surprisingly stimulating experiences.

A very unusual enquiry arrived from an unexpected quarter. The Austin Knight Advertising Agency had been commissioned by British Aerospace to plan a special programme for the launch of a new aircraft, and the time-scale for preparation was a precariously short one. The BAe 146-300 was hailed as the world's quietest passenger aeroplane and the launch was only a matter of weeks away at British Aerospace Hatfield on the outskirts of London. Agency planners latched on to the boast of the aircraft's muted engine noise, and decided that a choir performing an arrangement of Simon and Garfunkel's song, 'The Sound of Silence', would have a compelling impact at the launch. It was a strikingly original idea, but with the deadline quickly approaching, organisers had no musical arrangement and no choir. A male choir was the preferred option, and so the agency thought 'Wales'! Having decided that, they then placed their trust in the choir with a special track record, and the response was immediate and spontaneous. 'The greater the challenge, the greater the opportunity.' The work of arranging the piece was entrusted to the choir's accompanist, with the conductor transcribing the music into sol-fa notation. The turnaround to the commencement of rehearsing the piece was remarkably rapid, and the learning process had to take place during the choir's already busy schedule.

It wasn't a simple and straightforward arrangement either, as the brief from the advertising agency had been particularly specific and detailed. The unaccompanied piece was to be performed in the newly unveiled 'Assembly Hall', beginning with barely audible sounds as the aircraft remained in darkness. The music was to be one long, gradual *crescendo*, increasing in textural complexity as the plane slowly came into view, ending in a stirring climax as full floodlights illuminated the aircraft. Timing had to be precise for maximum impact. Everything worked splendidly, as the reaction of assembled international guests and the world's media testified. It was indeed a piece of pure theatre. As the plane was eventually taken out to prepare for its inaugural flight, it was inevitable that the choir was pressed into an impromptu concert inside the 'hanger', with encore following encore. For special visits such as this one, secretary John Davies meticulously prepared an itinerary booklet for distribution to each chorister. This particular one contained rather an unusual instruction:

> The secret of gaining maximum impact from a launch such as this, is that no-one is aware of the nature of the presentation to be staged on 1st May. To this end the advertising company have asked that we maintain a low profile in the hotels and on the morning of the launch, giving no indication as to the nature of our visit or that we are members of a choir.

Sinister subterfuge indeed! But from that day onwards, Côr Meibion Pontarddulais became known as 'the choir that launched a plane'!

Such flexibility in the choir's working practices was already known to Roger Waters from his liaison with the Bont years earlier during the recording of the sound track for Pink Floyd's film, *The Wall*. By 1987, the well-documented split within Pink Floyd had taken place, and Waters had by then branched out in new directions. Nevertheless his kudos as one of the world's most original and innovative rock musicians had continued unabated. He was now working on a new 'concept rock album' for Columbia Records, which had as its twin themes satellite communications dominating the future of mankind, and the obsession of global powers with capitalism and the free market. Such thought provoking themes and radical views were typical of Waters, and it was interesting that the resulting 'story line' for his album *Radio KAOS* was to have a close affinity with the south Wales mining community. It was hardly surprising therefore that he rekindled his successful association with the choir, returning again to the rehearsal room at Pontarddulais with his sophisticated technological gadgetry in order to discover the sounds he was after through a process of improvisation and experimentation, as he had done with *The Wall* five years earlier. A promotional video was also produced and filmed at Big Pit: the National Coal Museum. Choir members were required to dress as colliers and to have their faces blackened, an irony not lost on the choir's mining contingent. For the purpose of publicity and sales promotion, a performance tour was organised, and in an article appearing in the *Observer*, Waters is quoted as having said the following regarding an impending appearance in London:

> It's only 200 miles from Pontardoulais [*sic*]. I recorded the choir in the village school with a mobile unit. You can hear the birds singing outside in the background. I could not go happily to my grave without performing with the choir on stage. That will be a magic moment, to sing on stage with those guys.

Alas, 'those guys' are still waiting!

After eight years of service as chairman, Edward Morgan

relinquished the position to Brian Cousins in 1987, on the grounds of ill-health. Remarkably, Edward was to become one of the longest surviving heart transplant patients. Other experienced officers remained in post, bringing the administration a considerable degree of stability and consistency.

Unkind murmurings were surfacing at this time that the great competitive choir was in danger of turning its back on the world of eisteddfodau. Noel Davies did not take kindly to suggestions that a fear of losing the choir's unbeaten tag had manifested itself. The choir's absence from the National Eisteddfod during this period in its history has been explained in the previous chapter, and to some extent the so-called 'semi-nationals' had by this time declined somewhat in significance. Still, a point needed to be made, and the Miners' Eisteddfod at Porthcawl continued to provide a significant stage on which to do so. Not content to construct a programme of 'safe' music selected from a long-established repertoire, the conductor included a new piece by his old friend from Gowerton Grammar School days, Alun Hoddinott, Professor of Music at Cardiff University and composer of international repute. Hoddinott never compromised the challenge inherent in his music when writing for amateurs, and neither would he patronise them. Consequently, 'The Ballad of Green Broom' with its rhythmic vitality, complex syncopation and difficult six part cluster chords was as demanding a piece as any. The choir triumphed, the unbeaten record was extended and the taunts about a fear of losing were well and truly buried.

The enthusiasm for learning challenging new pieces by contemporary Welsh composers continued unabated, and another opportunity presented itself in 1988. For their traditional St David's Day concert the BBC commissioned Gareth Glyn to write a new piece for male choir and full orchestra. He decided upon a setting of Psalm 150, with its obvious musical connotations, and produced a remarkably colourful and lively anthem. The first performance was given at Cardiff's St David's Hall by Côr Meibion Pontarddulais and the BBC Welsh Symphony Orchestra, as it was then known, conducted by Owain Arwel Hughes. Both the composition and its performance were met with considerable critical acclaim, and Gareth Glyn was warm in his praise for the preparatory work of Noel Davies and his choir, acknowledging in a personal letter his admiration for the 'perfect conviction and confidence conveyed in the performance'.

Towards the end of that same year, the annual concert at the Brangwyn Hall took on a uniquely Pontarddulais flavour with Doreen, Patricia and Dennis O'Neill all joining the choir as guest artistes. Rarely if ever can one family have boasted such an astonishing array of top class singing talent, and it was no surprise that the evening attracted the attention of Opus 30, the television production company. They had been preparing a documentary on the choir during the preceding months and seized the opportunity of using this concert as a climax to their programme. Guest accompanist was Ingrid Surgenor, and it was invariably Ingrid, or Bryan Davies, who undertook such duties at annual concerts during the 1970s and 1980s. Their professionalism and outstanding musicianship were admired by the choir and audiences alike, and their friendship and commitment over the years were also greatly cherished.

A brief visit to Ireland was undertaken over the May bank holiday weekend in 1989 through the good auspices of the Dublin Welsh Male Choir, whose conductor, Keith Young, was himself a former member of Côr Meibion Pontarddulais. Successful concerts were given at the splendid venues of Christchurch and St Patrick's Cathedral.

Not since the choir's very earliest days had there been a deputy conductor, and there had never been an assistant accompanist either. Noel Davies's remarkable health record meant that he virtually never missed a rehearsal or concert. Over the years, if accompanists were not available for concerts, alternative emergency arrangements would be made. Noel Davies was comfortable with this position, though the accompanist of the time was not. To some extent, 1989 was a defining year with regards the music team at the helm. This was the year that saw Noel Davies's retirement from the post of headmaster at Cila Primary School on the outskirts of Swansea, where he had taught since the 1970s. Technically, at sixty-one years of age, it was an early retirement, but Noel harboured no intentions of retiring from his choral commitments. On the contrary, he was still full of life and enthusiasm, and now had even more time to devote to Côr Meibion Pontarddulais, with the result that the choir became busier still. Having left my post as Head of Music at Swansea's Mynyddbach School a couple of years earlier in order to take up a deputy headship at the newly established Welsh medium school, Ysgol Gyfun Gŵyr, pressures on my time were increasing significantly. The school was growing rapidly towards full capacity, and with two small daughters also seeking my attention, it was becoming increasingly difficult to devote the necessary time to one of the nation's most active choirs.

Some assistance was secured for accompanying at occasional rehearsals, though Noel was never completely at ease with such arrangements. Something else was also worrying him at this time, and he aired his views at the AGM. Whilst acknowledging the continuing success of his choir, he noted the need to attract young men to the choir's ranks. It was to become an on-going theme over the coming years, indeed up to the present day, and one to which we shall return in a later chapter. The problem of the accompanist remained unresolved, and although the general demeanour of the choir was re-invigorated with splendid new uniforms in 1990 – at a cost of £10,000 – I knew that my time as the choir's accompanist was coming to an end.

By 1991 it became impossible for me to continue, and I resigned after eighteen years of service, having had unforgettable experiences of performing, competing, broadcasting and recording with the choir at home and abroad. I was not allowed, nor would I have wished to disappear completely from the scene, and Noel Davies regularly asked me to compose or arrange music for the choir over the years to come. Llew Thomas, one of Noel's greatest friends and choir member of long standing, was another to resign at this time, as registrar. He had diligently kept important records of attendances at rehearsals and performances for a period of twenty-two years. Llew continued as an enthusiastic chorister.

Rarely does an established choral conductor give up the work in order to undertake duties as an accompanist. However, when Clive Phillips received an invitation from Noel Davies to take over as accompanist of Côr Meibion Pontarddulais, he accepted without hesitation – such was the attraction of working with the finest male choir in the land. Clive, a highly skilled pianist and organist was another product of Gowerton School's outstanding music department. Here was a man of considerable musical experience, having faced Côr y Bont in competition more than once as accompanist and deputy conductor of close rivals, Côr Meibion Llanelli. He had moved on to various conducting positions with the male choirs of Aberafon, Dunvant and Burry Port, from where he was eventually lured to the Bont. It was indeed a fortuitous appointment, and his association with Noel Davies brought with it a renewed sense of purpose and optimism for the future. The new partnership was to flourish for the next decade.

Pressures to repeat the Portugal experience of 1986 surfaced once more, and tentative arrangements were made to tour in 1992. Anxious to progress its international image further, the choir had commissioned the production of new glossy brochures for publicity purposes, securing worldwide distribution through a cluster of various agencies. One particular early response turned out to be the most striking of all – an invitation to sing in New Mexico, USA. Choir administrators knew very well the detailed financial planning needed in preparation for foreign tours, and realised that two overseas visits in close proximity would prove an impossibility. As a matter of courtesy it was acknowledged that the priority should be given to Portugal, even though firm arrangements had yet to be confirmed. When news eventually broke that a second Portuguese visit was not possible after all, disappointment was obviously tempered by the knowledge that with judicious planning, a tour to the United States was a distinct possibility. It was an indication of how much officers and committee had increasingly adopted a fully professional approach to choir matters that they advocated that the musical director and secretary should undertake a preliminary visit to New Mexico, with a brief of producing a detailed feasibility report. In the event, with Noel Davies wishing to give his full attention to a variety of commitments leading up to Christmas 1991, the task was left in the capable hands of John Davies. With his usual precision, he produced a lengthy and comprehensive report, which he distributed to all committee members for discussion.

The primary catalyst in the USA was Rhianwen Gerard, originally from Carno and a GI bride. She was the correspondence secretary of the New Mexico Welsh Society, and her husband George was at the time the immediate past President. Drawing its membership from a wide geographical area across the state of New Mexico, the society was based at Albuquerque. The second key player in terms of organisation within the United States was Dr James Irish, a member of the Board of Directors of the Durango Society of Cultural and Performing Arts, a body whose objective was to promote cultural diversity in music and art through education and performance. Jim Irish had visited a choir rehearsal during the summer of 1991, heard news of the proposed tour, and immediately expressed a wish to become actively involved.

Keen to ensure that all choir members would be kept abreast of developments as tour arrangements gathered pace, John Davies initiated a series of newsletters for distribution to all choristers. The first in the series emphasised the financial challenge involved in such an undertaking – the choir's most ambitious overseas visit to date. They were left in no doubt that fund-raising targets would be set for every chorister, whether or not they would be participating in the tour. Raising the necessary finance was to be a 'whole choir' responsibility, with an estimated £30,000 needed overall. As their usual busy schedule continued throughout 1992, choir officials became increasingly immersed in the time-consuming planning of the proposed tour, with constant liaison with the organisers in the USA.

Plans were eventually finalised for October 1993, with the preceding months of rehearsals polishing the tour repertoire integrated with preparations for other prestigious events. The annual St David's Day concert at Cardiff's St David's Hall saw the choir appear there for the third time in six years, and the choir also contributed to fund raising concerts for the Urdd National Eisteddfod, held in May on the doorstep in Gorseinon. The pre-tour concert, with the choir of Ysgol Gyfun Gŵyr, was given in September to a capacity audience at Gorseinon's Ebenezer chapel, and the time for the tour had arrived.

Clive Phillips was unable to travel, and the services of Alun Tregelles Williams were secured as accompanist for the tour, which commenced on 3 October, flying from Gatwick to Albuquerque, with a change of aircraft at Atlanta. The opening concert was given to a capacity audience at the Central Methodist Church, and greeted with rapturous applause and standing ovations. Hosted by members of the Welsh Society and friends, choristers also enjoyed various social occasions and opportunities of interaction with Welsh exiles and Americans alike. The venue for the second concert was the Civic Auditorium at Los Alamos, where the choir once again thrilled an enraptured audience. After an overnight stay, the choir travelled onwards to the engaging town of Durango in southern Colorado, famous for its cowboy connotations and complete with old style railroad terminus. New hosts warmly welcomed the choristers, and the tour's third concert was given at the Miller Auditorium, again to a capacity audience.

It was time for relaxation again, and the choristers assembled at the Trimble Hot Springs where they had an opportunity of enjoying the famous hot water spa. They moved on to a spectacular tour of the Grand Canyon before arriving at Gallup, where another successful concert was given at the Red Rocks Convention Centre. A tradition had been established during previous tours to Canada, Germany and Portugal, where the choir visited local schools, performing for children and young people. This tour was to be no exception, and the choir's next stop was Zuni Pueblo, where an informal concert was given to a large contingent of pupils in the Indian reservation there. In a stunning response, the youngsters gave a performance of a buffalo dance with native drum accompaniment.

Then it was back to Albuquerque and a resumption of friendships established at the commencement of the tour, where another concert was given to children and young people, on this occasion at the Sandia Preparatory School. On two occasions during the tour it was announced that the dates of the Pontarddulais Choir's visit would be noted in official records as 'Pontarddulais Male Choir Day', declarations that would forever note the choir's historic visit to a part of the world unaccustomed to the singing of Welsh male choirs. Modern technology enabled the transmission of news from New Mexico, Colorado and Arizona to reach home shores through the auspices of BBC Wales and the local radio station at Swansea Sound. Meticulous planning beforehand coupled with the undoubted musical success of the tour meant that the choir returned home with reputations enhanced. Securing significant sponsorship from the National Grid had proved vitally important for the financial success of the venture. As with previous tours, particularly those when choristers had been welcomed into the homes of hosts either directly or indirectly involved with the visit, a legacy was left in that communities had been inspired into renewed social interaction. Societies, particularly those with strong Celtic-exile influences, were reinvigorated with enthusiasm to maintain and develop their programmes of meetings and events over the years to come. It came as no surprise that requests for a return visit arrived virtually immediately.

It is worth re-emphasising at this point the obvious camaraderie that exists within the choir's ranks, derived from years of singing and performing, travelling and socialising together. Lifelong friendships have been sustained in this way. There has always been a very real sense of 'family' or reciprocal pastoral care, and this latest tour served to underline this in a challenging set of circumstances. No fewer than three choir members were hospitalised during the tour, raising obvious concerns amongst fellow choristers and families back home. In that related practical and administrative issues were overcome flawlessly is a testament to the efficiency of officers, but equally importantly the worries of the sick patients were alleviated by the uplifting support of choristers in general, at what was for them a particularly traumatic time.

This was a period of key administrative personnel changes. John Davies relinquished his position as secretary, taking over the Chair from Brian Cousins who had given six years of unstinting and loyal service in his own inimitably unassuming manner. In terms of sustained paperwork, the secretary's time-consuming responsibilities are probably the most daunting, and once again the choir was extremely fortunate in the appointment of Winston Price to the post. Côr Meibion Pontarddulais had discovered within its ranks another fine servant.

With the exception of the Miners' Eisteddfod in Porthcawl in 1987, when Noel Davies wanted to prove a point, the choir had not competed since the Swansea National of 1982. Now, in 1994, the National was returning to the locality in Neath, and one of the test pieces for the 'Chief' male choir competition was Schubert's remarkable 'Song of the Spirits over the Waters'. The choir had first tackled this challenging work back in 1967, and had also sung it at the Bro Myrddin National Eisteddfod in 1974, a performance considered by Noel Davies himself to have been the best ever at a National Eisteddfod. It is not only a lengthy piece, but divides into eight vocal parts. In terms of its composition it is cleverly and subtly understated, yet making considerable demands on the musicality and sensitivity of any male choir attempting to convey its romantic mysticism. Months of painstaking preparation eventually ended with the realisation that no other choir had entered the competition, thus repeating the circumstances encountered once before at the Ammanford National of 1970. It was a consummate performance eliciting highly complimentary plaudits from the panel of distinguished adjudicators, and yet there was a feeling of anticlimax and frustration. However, the remarkable record had been extended with an eleventh win, in what was to be Noel Davies's final attempt at the National. He was to turn his attention to another eisteddfod, as we shall see.

In the meantime another overseas tour, the choir's ninth, was already in the advanced planning stage. Having visited eastern Canada on two occasions in the 1970s, it was now to be the turn of the Rocky Mountains and the western seaboard to sample the choir's musical pedigree. The experienced administrative team forged ahead with the complex arrangements, setting appropriate financial targets for an eighteen-day tour in May 1996. Before looking more closely at the details of that visit, it is worth recalling some other matters of interest from 1996. In terms of continuity of service, the fact that Alun Davies had held the post of treasurer since 1971 was of enormous benefit to the choir. It was he who had carefully managed financial matters with professionalism, always in an unassuming and unpretentious manner. It was he also who had masterminded the financial logistics of all overseas tours, apart from the very first visit to Sweden. Now, after a quarter of a century of unbroken service, the choir enthusiastically acknowledged his considerable contribution with a special presentation.

Another long-serving figurehead, from the very beginning of the choir's thirty-six-year existence, had been hitherto its only president, Ieuan M Williams. For him, 1996 brought the disappointment, because of ill-health, of failing to attend the annual concert, and that for the only time since the very first in the series in 1962, in those days at the old 'Tiv' in Pontarddulais.

There were also lighter moments in 1996, one of which saw the choir perform at a rather unusual venue. Broadcasting agencies are well known for coming up with unusually striking ideas for their programmes, and on this occasion the brainwave was to invite Côr Meibion Pontarddulais to sing in the Swansea valley's famous Dan yr Ogof Caves. Television producers were adamant that the choir was to perform in one of the more visually stunning caverns, on ground sloping towards one of the many underground lakes. But where was the musical director to be positioned in order to conduct the choir satisfactorily? Despite being dressed immaculately in a dinner suit and bow tie, Noel Davies was invited to don a pair of wellington boots and stand in the lake, albeit shallow. No-one batted an eyelid; it was after all television, and TV producers knew what they were doing. Legend has it that as the fine sounds of 'Gwahoddiad' emanated from the choir in the rich acoustic of the caves, Noel was seen to be slowly sinking. On completion of the recording, one chorister was heard to say, "Thank God 'Gwahoddiad' didn't have a fourth verse, or Noel would have disappeared for ever!"

There were no such problems on the Canadian tour, which ran smoothly from beginning to end. Over preceding months the choir had recorded two new compact discs in readiness for international sales. The first was a compilation of hymns that included contributions by Harry Secombe, Moira Anderson and the Choir of Guildford Cathedral as well as the Bont. The other, *The Old Rugged Cross*, was the usual eclectic mix long associated with the choir, varying in style from the rousing 'Alexander's Ragtime Band' to Faure's sublime 'Cantique de Jean Racine'. The guest accompanist for this latest tour was D Hugh Jones, who was once again renewing his long-standing association with Côr y Bont. The choir was indeed fortunate to secure the services of such an outstanding musician at comparatively short notice. Hugh had been the choir's official accompanist at the beginning of the 1970s, and had frequently helped out periodically over the succeeding years. His distinguished contribution to the choir was acknowledged with the award of life membership.

Co-ordinator of the tour on the Canadian side was Yvonne Evans of Sidney, British Columbia, who liaised admirably with a contingent of Welsh Societies at Calgary, Vernon, Vancouver and Mid Island. As with previous tours there were welcome opportunities of blending formal concerts with more informal social occasions, and whilst travelling from one centre to another there were exciting opportunities of enjoying spectacular scenery. The opening concert at Calgary's Grace Church was followed the next morning with a journey to Canmore, passing through the beautiful countryside of Banff and Jasper and past the crystal clear waters of Lake Louise. The next stop was Vernon where the Welsh Society had arranged a Civic Reception for representatives of the choir, and a lively party following the concert at the town's Recreational Centre. The next leg of the tour involved a long journey by coach and ferry in order to reach Vancouver Island, where two further concerts were given at the Royal Theatre in Victoria and at the Cowichan Theatre in Duncan. Finally, the choir retraced its steps to Vancouver and experienced the enthusiastic welcome of the Welsh Society there, giving the last concert of the tour at the city's United Church.

Once again the choir had been privileged to sing in splendid venues and to capacity audiences whose enthusiasm and appreciation had been inspirational. Native Canadians and Welsh expatriates alike had often travelled considerable distances in order to reach the concerts and experience the unique sounds and emotionally charged performances. The ninth overseas tour had proved to be another resounding success, and it is a measure of the choristers' unbounded stamina that as well as completing their official obligations in a packed itinerary, they still managed to squeeze in some sight-seeing, which included the Calgary Winter Olympic Park, Harrison Hot Springs, the Victoria Parliament Buildings as well as the beautiful Butchart Gardens.

The question of how to maintain momentum within any organisation is an interesting one. The challenge in this respect for a high-achieving choir is particularly real. So many well known choirs have reached admirable peaks, only to be followed by deep troughs. Others have seen numbers dwindle as enthusiasm waned. Some fine choral societies of the past, who contributed so much to our national tradition, have literally disappeared. On the part of some male choirs, there has been a degree of compromise with regards repertoire, abandoning classical works of substance as well as the new music of contemporary composers, for the more light-weight material designed for so called 'easy listening'. William Mathias once said that he considered himself particularly fortunate in that he literally enjoyed all kinds of music. Noel Davies was not averse to introducing pop songs, songs from the shows or so called 'lollipops' into the repertoire, but he also remained firm to his commitment of expanding the musical horizons of his choristers. This philosophy, coupled with his own relentless personal drive, was the undoubted way of maintaining momentum as far as the Bont was concerned. Though evident from the very beginning, this is particularly exemplified at this point in the choir's history, when in 1997, as well as including rarely performed works by Schubert, Mendelssohn, Gounod and Max Bruch in its concert programmes, the choir also mastered fifteen new choral arrangements of Gershwin songs for a recording on the Carlton label, described on the disc's inlay card as a 'definitive collection performed by a choir acknowledged in Wales to be one of the finest ever produced in the Principality'.

As well as musical challenge in terms of repertoire, there was also another important factor in maintaining momentum. Noel Davies had always been unwavering in his conviction that preparing diligently and conscientiously for the competitive arena was a means of honing the collective skills of his singers and of pushing them hard in terms of standards. However, the choir had experienced disappointment at the National of 1994 as the only entrants in the competition. Were other choirs staying away when news broke that Côr Meibion Pontarddulais would be competing? Noel had always been a great admirer of the Llangollen International Eisteddfod, and over the years frequently travelled to the festival to hear the male choir competition on the final Saturday. However, the Eisteddfod authorities placed a restriction on the number of singers, and Pontarddulais was too large a choir to compete. When the rules changed though, and the stipulation simply stated a competition for male choirs 'of not less than 30 voices', Noel signalled that when circumstances allowed, he intended taking his choir to Llangollen.

The choir's schedule for 1998 was already packed with several concerts involving long journeys to various English counties. There was also a prestigious invitation to take part in the opening ceremony of the NATO Reserve Officers Congress in the Brighton Centre in July – a direct clash with Llangollen as it happened. The Congress takes place annually in one of the NATO countries, and 1998 was the turn of the United Kingdom. As well as guests from all fifteen NATO countries, there were also representatives from Eastern Europe, Australia and South Africa. This explains why there was to be no attempt at Llangollen at this time, but there were certainly clues in the programme of the annual concert later that year suggesting that 1999 could be the year for the choir's first appearance at the International Eisteddfod.

Llangollen had developed an identical test piece format for all its choral competitions. This required singing one piece selected by the Eisteddfod itself, an own choice by a composer born between 1700 and 1900, as well as a further own choice of a twentieth century piece by a composer of the competing choir's own country. The total performance time for the own-choice pieces was not to exceed nine minutes. As well as some rarely heard part songs by Schubert, the annual concert programme in 1998 included Mathias's 'Gloria', the choir's own commission from 1970, the 'Prisoners' Chorus' from Beethoven's opera *Fidelio*, the 'Soldier's Chorus' from

Bellini's *Norma* and large scale choruses by Richter and Gounod. It looked as though Noel Davies was polishing a sub-set of pieces from which a selection could be made for the following year's Llangollen competition.

But before Llangollen, in the late spring of 1999, there was another important engagement to fulfil, and a very different one at that. It had been some time since the choir had worked with rock musicians, even though the opportunity of singing live with Roger Waters and Pink Floyd had never actually materialised. However, the group of the moment, in an international context, was the Welsh band Catatonia, with Cerys Mathews as lead singer. The choir combined with the group in a gig at Margam Park, joining in a performance of 'Mulder and Scully' to the delight of an ecstatic audience of over thirty thousand young people. Hitherto this was the largest audience ever for the choir in a single event, and the excitement of the day wasn't at all soured by the torrential downpours throughout the concert.

Inevitably, the choice of programme for Llangollen proved critical. As well as the stipulated test piece – a motet from the renaissance period – Noel included the Beethoven operatic chorus, but because of the time restriction on the overall performance, rather than choose the lengthy Mathias piece on which the choir had been working, he decided on a revival of Hoddinott's shorter 'Green Broom' as representative of a twentieth century piece by a Welsh composer. The competition was fiercely contested with several previous winners at Llangollen in the line up. The highest mark for a single piece went to Côr y Bont for their performance of the 'Prisoners' Chorus', with the adjudicators commenting that 'the subtle gradations of dynamics, coupled with the controlled timbres, represent male choral singing at its best'. But alas, the adjudicators' enthusiasm was not sustained for the final piece, though some eyebrows were raised on hearing their views articulated on Hoddinott's

'Green Broom'. It seemed that criticism was reserved for the piece rather than the performance when chair of the panel, Conan Castle, commented, 'An undemanding piece that poses little challenge to the singers and few rewards for the listeners'. Many would have vehemently disagreed.

Winners for the second year running were the Colne Valley Male Choir of Huddersfield, closely followed by Côr Godre'r Aran, winners in 1996, with Côr y Bont coming in a creditable third. It was the first time that Côr Meibion Pontarddulais had failed to win a competition since the National Eisteddfod of 1967, and neither the fact that they had come close nor the invitation to sing at the prestigious evening concert softened the blow. It was a critical time in the choir's history for several reasons.

On the turn of the new millennium, several factors combined to create a deeply melancholy atmosphere. Noel's wife, Joan, had been a stalwart supporter of the choir from its very origins in the Bont Youth Club at the beginning of the 1960s. She had been a tower of strength to Noel throughout the years, and now she was succumbing to the cruel grip of Alzheimer's in its advanced stages. Noel's own health was slowly deteriorating, and for someone who had very rarely indeed failed to attend a rehearsal or concert in almost forty years, it came as a tremendous shock that he missed the 1999 annual concert because of illness. Clive Phillips deputised admirably at short notice, only becoming aware of the situation on the morning of the concert.

The health of the choir's president, Ieuan Williams, had never recovered from several reverses over recent years, and he passed away in the New Year of 2000. A kind and wise man, with a keen sense of humour, he had proved an influential figurehead over almost four decades, representing the choir at official functions and often travelling with the choristers on foreign tours. As a Bont boy himself, he knew many of the choristers personally. He would inevitably turn up at a

The first official photograph, 1962, taken in the grounds of Pontarddulais Secondary Modern School (now Pontarddulais Primary). Always regarded as the choir's home base, rehearsals are still held twice weekly at the school.

Back in Pontarddulais following the first 'National' victory at Llandudno, 1963.

Pontarddulais Welfare Hall, formerly the Tivoli Cinema, 1965. On display are the record number of trophies won that year. For the first time ever, a male choir had swept the board at all major Welsh competitive festivals – Pontrhydfendigaid, Cardigan, the Miners' Eisteddfod at Porthcawl as well as the National Eisteddfod at Newtown.

A rehearsal in the Swedish countryside, 1966. The choir's first overseas tour.

The first of many appearances at the splendid Birmingham Town Hall, 1966.

On behalf of the Ladies Section, Joan Davies (wife of Noel Davies) presents Tom Coles, chairman, with a contribution towards choir funds, 1967.

Barry National Eisteddfod, 1968.

The touring Pakistan cricket side visit a rehearsal, 1974.

Royal Albert Hall, 1974.

Cardigan National Eisteddfod, 1976.

Tour of eastern Canada, 1977.

Rheindahlen, Germany, 1979. The Rheindahlen Military Complex, also known as Joint Headquarters (JHQ) functioned as the main headquarters for British forces in Germany. On this tour, and again on a subsequent tour the following year, the choir stayed at the nearby Wildenrath RAF Base.

Noel Davies meets HRH The Queen Mother during the opening concert of the recently completed St David's Hall in Cardiff, 1983.

Noel Davies, Joan Davies, George Guest, Gwen Williams, Ieuan Williams at the twenty-fifth anniversary dinner.

São Carlos Theatre, Lisbon, Portugal, 1986.

British Aerospace, Hatfield, London, 1987.

Dublin, 1989.

Preparing for S4C's *Noson Lawen*, 1989.

Noel Davies presents a gift to Llew Thomas on his retirement as registrar after a period of twenty-two years, 1991.

Brangwyn Hall, Swansea, 1992. The first official photograph with recently appointed accompanist, Clive Phillips. The Brangwyn Hall has been the venue for the choir's annual concert since 1970.

Tour of New Mexico, Colorado and Arizona, USA, 1993.

Wembley Recording Studios, 1995.

Outside the Victoria Parliament Buildings, Canada, 1996.

Dan yr Ogof Caves, 1996.

Ebenezer Chapel, Gorseinon, 2000.

Civic Reception 2002.

Clive Phillips holds the National Eisteddfod trophy for the first time, Meifod, 2003. The choir's victory was dedicated to the memory of founder conductor, Noel Davies, who had sadly passed away only a week earlier.

Eric Jones installed as president, 2004.

New York City Central Labor Council, 2007.

Capitol Hill, Washington, 2007.

Founder members honoured with life membership, 2008.

On stage at the Cardiff National Eisteddfod, 2008.

Secretary Lyn Anthony presents Howard Johns, concert organiser, with a token of the choir's appreciation, Fuengirola, Spain, 2010.

final rehearsal to wish the choir well before an important competition, and it was he who had written a history of the choir's first twenty-five years in his incomparably eloquent style. His old friend, Professor Emeritus Sir Glanmor Williams, paid the final tribute at the funeral before the choir sang Bruch's setting of Psalm 23. A change in the choir's constitution at this time established the principle of appointing life vice presidents, and Ieuan's widow Gwen was the first to be invested with this very special honour, in recognition of her loyal support to her late husband, and to the choir.

By this time also, Noel had lost some of his very closest friends in the choir, and the number of choristers briefly dipped below a hundred for the first time since 1962. In adversity Noel Davies's fierce determination shone through, possibly a defence mechanism to combat the sadness that enveloped him at this time. There would be a second attempt at Llangollen. The test piece this time was the 'Pilgrims' Chorus' from Wagner's *Tannhauser*, which the choir had first prepared as long ago as 1965, for the Newtown National Eisteddfod. However, their success then was not to be repeated at Llangollen on this occasion, and it was their great Welsh rivals, Côr Godre'r Aran, who took the spoils by a whisker, with Côr y Bont in second place. It was the choir's fortieth anniversary year, and a victory at Llangollen would have put the icing on the celebratory cake, but it was not to be. It was a reflection of the choir's high standard and competitive reputation that coming a very close second at Llangollen was not considered good enough. Where would the choir now go with an obviously ailing musical director at the helm?

Before the end of the year, there was a splendid anniversary dinner with former accompanist, now distinguished international conductor, Wyn Davies, returning to propose a toast to 'Mr Noel Davies and the

Pontarddulais Male Choir'. I had the privilege of responding on behalf of guests, and in his own speech, Noel Davies, despite the deterioration in his health, showed that he had lost none of his spark or his humour. At the end of the year Brian Cousins returned to the Chair vacated by John Davies.

The gathering dark clouds of recent years stubbornly refused to disperse, and on New Year's Day 2001, Noel's wife Joan passed away. They had no children of their own, and Noel himself had been an only child. It was a difficult time despite the support of his closest friends within the choir and their families. Undoubtedly this severe blow would have a further detrimental effect on his deteriorating health. He sought advice on whether he should retire, but deep down, a burning ambition remained. He knew that his choir was good enough to win at Llangollen, and he was determined to have one last shot at it.

The test piece for 2001 was the 'Bandits' Chorus' from Verdi's *Ernani*, and to complete Côr y Bont's challenging programme, Noel added 'Si Hwi' (Eric Jones), 'Y Pren ar y Bryn' (William Mathias) and 'The Last Words of David' (Randall Thompson). The conductor's determination to sing the Verdi chorus in the original language resulted in procuring the services of an Italian language coach in order to refine the pronounciation of the singers. The performances went well, and when the chairman of the adjudicating panel, distinguished American choral conductor Dr Andre J Thomas, began his adjudication of the Bont's programme with, 'What a sound!' it was evident that the International Trophy would be theirs at the third attempt. Thomas, also speaking on behalf of fellow adjudicators Jean Stanley Jones and Ralph Allwood, went on to praise the choir's clear diction and good balance and noted 'its great sensitivity for such a large ensemble'. Froncysyllte, three times previous winners at Llangollen, were the runners up on this occasion with Warrington Male Choir in third place. Winners of every choral category at the Eisteddfod traditionally competed against each other on the final evening of the festival for the title of 'Choir of the World'. Côr Meibion Pontarddulais were joined by mixed choir winners, the Sombor Choral Society of Yugoslavia, female choir winners, the Choir of Estonian Choral Conductors, and chamber choir winners, the Australia Voices. Although the title went to the Estonian choir, nothing could detract from the joy of winning the male choir competition earlier in the day, though it was a very frail Noel Davies who went to the stage to collect the trophy that had until then proved so elusive.

Within three months of the Llangollen victory the choir were undertaking a concert tour of southern Spain. For the first time on an overseas tour, Noel Davies was unable to travel due to ill health, and it became clear that continuing to direct such a remarkably busy choir would ultimately prove impossible for him. As Clive Phillips had done so competently in the annual concert of 1999, he once more took over conducting duties, and the choir was fortunate enough to engage the services of the young and talented David Last as a guest accompanist. It was evident from the rousing success of this tour that the future musical leadership of the choir had been glimpsed during this week on the Costa Blanca. Once again on an overseas visit the choir was privileged to sing at prestigious venues, renowned for the splendour of their architecture and the quality of their acoustics. The opening concert was given at Torrevieja's Parroquia Immaculada Concepción to a capacity audience of over 1,400 including a large contingent of British emigrants. The second concert at the new Palacio de la Musica, part of the Coservatoire de la Musica, was also a sell out. There was also a capacity audience at the final concert given at Iglesia San Martin in Callosa de Segura, a fine church designated as one of Spain's national monuments, and dating from the sixteenth century. At this concert the choir was joined by the Coral Callosa San Martin, one of Spain's foremost mixed choirs. The performances of Côr Meibion Pontarddulais were greeted with rapturous receptions at all three venues, and the year 2001 had become another during which the choir's international credentials had been enhanced even further.

By the end of November Noel Davies was once more back at the helm for the annual concert at the Brangwyn Hall. Joining Jennifer Rees Davies and Eirian James as guest artistes were 'Y Tri Baswr' with their accompanist Eirian Owen, thus cementing a special relationship that had developed between Côr y Bont and Côr Godre'r Aran over recent years, particularly at Llangollen. The triumvirate of basses, Tom Evans (Gwanas), Trebor Lloyd Evans and Iwan Wyn Parry were all members of Godre'r Aran, and Eirian of course was the choir's inspirational musical director, and vocal coach to all three singers. It was a musical feast and, as it transpired, a fitting climax to Noel Davies's career with the choir, for within a matter of weeks he had decided to relinquish his post. Poignantly, he chose his seventy fourth birthday, 6 January 2002, to write his letter of resignation:

> This is probably the most difficult letter I'll ever write... I wish to retire as Musical Director of the Choir. I've had 41 glorious years of music making with the finest choir you could have. We've had great successes over the years, especially this year, and I've taken the choir as far as I can... I will miss it terribly. With Joan's encouragement and support, it's been my life since 1960.

The resignation was to take effect when the choir broke for its traditional summer recess in August, which effectively meant that Noel would complete forty-two years of service. In a celebratory dinner and dance held in his honour on 27 September 2002, fittingly held at Swansea's Brangwyn

Hall, he was installed as the choir's new president and as conductor emeritus. His natural successor was Clive Phillips, the choir's accompanist since 1991, and David Last, the young man who had stepped in at the last moment as accompanist on the Spanish tour the previous year was now appointed Clive's successor as the choir's official principal accompanist. A native of Northallerton in Yorkshire, David was affectionately given the Welsh nickname 'Dai Diwethaf' by choristers. He broke a long-standing tradition, as every one of his predecessors had a direct connection with Gowerton School. Another tradition was coming to an end as well in that both the musical director and the accompanist were freelance musicians and were involved in other musical activities and organisations in addition to their duties with Côr y Bont. This was a natural trend as a new generation of talented musicians confidently strove to make a living from a variety of music-making activities. The organist John M Davies was also added to the musical team at this time. With a wide-ranging musical interest extending from jazz to amateur operatics, he had appropriately been Clive Phillips's first organ tutor.

This was a pivotal moment in the history of the choir. Noel Davies's name had been synonymous with that of Côr Meibion Pontarddulais from the very beginning, and although he remained as a father figure on the fringes, there was now a new regime in place, both musically and administratively as Brian Cousins relinquished the Chair to his successor, Ian Lloyd. Long standing conductors had famously retired from other well known choirs over the years, and often the change in personnel had led to a decline, not only in musical standards but also in general enthusiasm, with a resulting loss of impetus. In the particular case of Côr y Bont, the very highest choral standards had been set, and its reputation was second to none. What would the future hold?

4

A NEW REGIME
(2003-09)

AFICIONADOS OF THE MALE choir world watched, listened and waited. The new musical director was expected to take time to consolidate, and certainly to keep a low profile with regards the competitive arena. After all, Côr Meibion y Bont's unbeaten tag at the National Eisteddfod went back as far as 1968. It was anticipated that Clive Phillips would devote a year or two to finding his feet, gradually freeing himself from the intimidating shadow of his illustrious predecessor. But in a ten-year association with Noel Davies, during which the two had developed a close friendship as well as a strong musical bond, could that element of stubbornness, so often associated with the choir's founder, have rubbed off on the protégé? Stubbornness here of course refers to that positive attribute of focused determination and passion, an uncompromising and resolute perseverance, rather than self-opinionated bigotry. With obvious courage, Clive Phillips announced that the choir would compete at the Maldwyn National Eisteddfod of 2003.

Before that, however, there were administrative issues to be addressed and financial challenges to be met. A newsletter for choristers dated May 2003 pointed to the increased running costs of the choir. An imminent short concert tour to Jersey was to cost in the region of £32,000, primarily because of air travel and hotel charges. Projections for the annual concert later in the year indicated fees of £4,000 for artistes with further expenditure for the hire of the hall and its staff. The weekly tote, which had served the choir well for over forty years, was to be revised in order to increase revenue, and the committee's efforts to secure sponsorship led to a major deal with Brecon Carreg Natural Mineral Water at this time. Arrangements with regards charges for concert performances were not to change, with the newsletter affirming, 'Although the choir seeks to cover its costs when undertaking engagements, there is a danger that we could price ourselves out of the market if we introduced a fee on top of expenses.'

All successful concert tours have a dedicated resident organiser and trouble-shooter at the destination, and in the case of Côr y Bont's visit to Jersey in June it was Clive Phillips's sister Haulwen who undertook responsibility for the arrangements. Everything ran smoothly with the choir performing to capacity audiences at the St James Arts Centre and the St Helier Methodist Centre. On arriving home, the choir realised that it was only a matter of weeks before the National Eisteddfod, and all minds were now concentrated on the impending challenge.

Following the custom set by Ieuan Williams over the years, Noel Davies, as the choir's president attended one of the final rehearsals before the Eisteddfod to wish the choir well. Conscious of the previous eleven victories at the National, he exhorted the choir to 'Make it a twelfth' as he hoped to join them on their eisteddfod visit, on this occasion as their most ardent supporter. Exactly a week before the competition though, Noel passed away at his home in Kingsbridge, Gorseinon, whilst watching on television the opening competitions of the Eisteddfod's first day. It was a sad and contemplative choir that travelled to Meifod on Saturday 9 August 2003.

The National Eisteddfod had changed its format for choral competitions and Côr Meibion Pontarddulais chose to enter the competition for male choirs 'of any size over 20'. Choirs in this competition were required to present a balanced programme of up to fifteen minutes in length to include a piece by a Welsh composer from 1980 onwards. These requirements were reminiscent of Llangollen, and in fact Côr y Bont included some of the pieces that had brought them success at the International Eisteddfod two years previously. To these were added Gareth Glyn's stirring and uplifting 'Heriwn, wynebwn y wawr', a choice that appropriately seemed to herald a new era for the choir, and the ultimate dawning of a new day. There were also other echoes of Llangollen as great rivals Froncysyllte once more appeared as opponents. Côr Meibion Llangwm and Côr Meibion y Penrhyn were the other two competing choirs.

The competition witnessed some excellent singing by all choirs, but one choir was determined to 'make it a twelfth', not so much for themselves, or even for their new musical director, but for their founder conductor. On behalf of the adjudicating panel, Brian Hughes concluded his remarks with rarely heard accolades at National Eisteddfod choral competitions:

A choir of splendid voices singing with power and tenderness. Their mastery of choral technique is assured and their imagination is on fire at all times. This is the finest male choir singing that I have heard for many years.

After the presentations of prizes, Brian Hughes returned to the stage to pay an emotional tribute to the late Noel Davies. The victory was dedicated to his memory, although celebrations were set aside as the choir travelled home to sing at his funeral at St Catherine's Church, Gorseinon, on Monday 11 August. Many of Noel's friends joined choir members back at the Pontarddulais Rugby Club after the committal service at Swansea Crematorium, and expressed their collective emotions in the best way they knew. They sang.

It was the end of one era and the beginning of another and, with Brian Hughes's endorsement ringing in their ears, the choir could look forward to the future with confidence. However, his superlatives also challenged the choir in terms of maintaining its standards and enhancing its reputation. How could the programme for 2004 contribute to this? In addition to the choir's regular busy schedule of concert performances, it would compete both at Llangollen and at the Newport National Eisteddfod. No pressure there then!

Before the attempt at the 'double' the choir had decided to commemorate their founder by establishing an annual memorial concert, the first of which was held at Pontarddulais in May 2004. It was the evening when a new President was also installed, and although I had never expected such an invitation, I was only too happy to acknowledge the honour and accept with gratitude and pride.

The challenge awaiting the choir was immense. Their record at the National was second to none, and they had already proved that they were good enough to win at Llangollen. But would victory at both festivals, and within one month of each other, prove one step too far? The test piece at Llangollen was Orlando di Lasso's French madrigal 'Bonjour, mon Coeur', a work first introduced by Noel Davies into the choir's repertoire prior to the first Canadian tour of 1973. To this was added Mathias's 'Gloria', which had served the choir well in several previous competitions, and Brian Hughes's vibrant 'Bywyd y Bugail'. English 'big guns' and Llangollen regulars, Colne Valley, Warrington and Bolsterstone were all formidable opponents, as were Welsh giants Llanelli, Dunvant, and inevitably Froncysyllte who had experienced numerous successes at Llangollen in previous years. It was to prove another Llangollen triumph for Côr y Bont, with the wonderfully named, and excellent young Welsh choir, Côr Undebol Ar Ôl Tri coming a close second. Comparatively small in terms of numbers, this choir had made its mark in several important competitions over previous years, with some outstanding performances. Third place went to England's Wessex Male Choir. Once again, after an intense competition during the day, the winning male choir was expected to face the Choir of the World competition on the same evening. Some commentators have expressed the view that it is this requirement that has prevented a male choir from taking this prestigious title since its inception in 1987. Côr y Bont joined Swedish choirs Mariakoren and Ad Libitum as well as the English barbershop choir, the Cambridge Chord Company, in this battle of winners in each of the Eisteddfod's choral categories. The title went to the Cambridge Chord Company, whose pedigree in the world of barbershop singing was undoubted as winners of many important competitions. Some had viewed them as unlikely winners beforehand, primarily arguing that their restricted repertoire in terms of style would count against them. However, their ability to communicate their infectious enthusiasm to the audience obviously also impressed the panel of adjudicators on this occasion.

As far as Côr y Bont was concerned, the first important element of their challenging mission had been achieved with victory in Llangollen's male choir competition – the first leg of the attempted 'double'. The National Eisteddfod at Newport was now only a matter of weeks away, and although the easier option would have been to utilise all of the music sung at Llangollen as test pieces in Newport, Clive Phillips, apart from retaining 'Bywyd y Bugail', had decided on a different programme. The music, however, was not unfamiliar to choristers of long standing, for added to the recent favourite 'Heriwn, Wynebwn y Wawr', was Randall Thompson's 'Last Words of David' first introduced into the repertoire in 1965, and Viadana's motet 'Ave verum corpus', which the choir had first learned for the annual concert of 1979. The elusive double was secured, and indeed enhanced with the announcement that the newly established title of 'Côr yr Ŵyl' – the best choir from all of the Eisteddfod's week of choral competitions, was to be awarded to Côr Meibion Pontarddulais. This was indeed a unique achievement, Pontarddulais becoming the first choir to win at Llangollen and be crowned 'Côr yr Ŵyl' at the National Eisteddfod in the same year.

The panel of choral adjudicators at the Newport National was an interesting one, comprising Gwyn L Williams, who was himself closely associated with the Llangollen Eisteddfod; Swansea born Huw Williams, sub-organist at St Paul's Cathedral; and Adrian Partington, Director of the BBC National Chorus of Wales. As Chair of the panel for the male choir competition, Gwyn L Williams offered valuable and valid advice to male choirs performing renaissance period motets, which had been favourite test pieces in countless eisteddfod competitions over the years. For example, Pontarddulais had sung Kerle's 'Agnus Dei' in their first National victory in 1963. Gwyn Williams pointed out that the editions of such music by his namesake and Llangollen predecessor W S Gwynn Williams, very often used in Wales, were now outdated. Modern research and editing techniques had led to more authentic performances of catholic music from the sixteenth century, invariably emphasising a brisker tempo and a more robust overall sound. These are important lessons to learn. With his second piece of advice, this time to the Eisteddfod establishment, Gwyn L Williams risked the wrath of some by advocating that vocal music ought to be sung at the festival in the original language, rather than adhere strictly to the 'all-Welsh rule'. Exceptions to this rule, often unexplained, had periodically occurred. As mentioned in a previous chapter, the 'Agnus Dei' at the chief male voice competition in 1963, for example, had been sung in Latin. Gwyn L Williams's view expressed at Newport was met with audible booing from some sections of the audience. Others would have agreed with the sentiments expressed.

A truly remarkable year concluded with the annual concert at the Brangwyn Hall when the choir was joined by rapidly rising star Katherine Jenkins, the Richard Williams Singers and the young violinist Amir Bisengaliev for a memorable feast of music. There were two important changes of choir officers in 2004. Industrious secretary over the past eleven years, Winston Price handed over the reigns to Lyn Anthony, and Alun Davies, treasurer since 1971, relinquished his financial responsibilities, with Bryan Davies taking over. It was a significant moment in that the duties of key officers had now been transferred to a new generation. It was also a sign of the times that the post of treasurer was now to be a 'non-singing' role.

One 'spin-off' from the Llangollen Eisteddfod was the close friendship struck up between Côr y Bont and the Wessex Male Choir, and the Noel Davies Memorial Concert of 2005 saw the English choir taking part together with the Welsh soprano Iona Jones. The Bont would return to the Swindon area for a reciprocal visit and concert in 2006; such is the camaraderie between male choirs. At the memorial concert, Winston Price's contribution as secretary was acknowledged with the award of life membership, and administrative stalwarts John Davies and Alun Davies, whose contributions as officers from the choir's very earliest days were immeasurable, were invested as life vice presidents. This was also the year that saw Côr Meibion Pontarddulais sing to its largest live audience ever. The occasion was the Six Nations Rugby Championship game between Wales and England at Cardiff's Millennium Stadium, with the choir entertaining the huge crowd before the match, and leading the singing of the national anthem. The singing must have been inspirational as Wales recorded an historic win, and went on to achieve their first Grand Slam since 1978.

Côr Meibion Pontarddulais had competed at the National Eisteddfod on its visit to Swansea in 1964 and again in 1982, when the festival on both occasions had been held in the attractive grounds of Singleton Park. The venue for the Eisteddfod's visit to Swansea in 2006 was altogether different. It would be held on the bleak site of the demolished Felindre Tinplate Works, a stone's throw from Pontarddulais itself. Thinking of the significantly large number of past and present choir members who had toiled there over several decades, how strange it was to contemplate welcoming the 'National' to the site of that old works. To the favourites, Mathias's 'Gloria' and Gareth Glyn's 'Heriwn, Wynebwn y Wawr', Clive Phillips added a new piece, 'Nos o Haf', by the choir's president, thus compiling a programme of challenging contemporary Welsh music for the competition. Disappointingly, arch rivals Côr Meibion Llanelli were the only opponents, but not only did Côr y Bont extend its remarkable record of victories at the nation's premier competitive festival to fourteen, but the choir was also once again voted 'Choir of the Festival'. This was from a field of over thirty choirs that had competed enthusiastically during the week in competitions of a very high standard. As the Eisteddfod reached its climax on the final afternoon, emotions were mixed as Clive Phillips received a special trophy as the conductor of 'Côr yr Ŵyl', – a baton presented in memory of Noel Davies by his god-daughter, Gill Evans, the first in a series to be commissioned annually by her.

Having visited Ireland at the request of the Dublin Welsh Male Choir in 1989, Côr y Bont now received an invitation to return, on this occasion to help the Dublin choir celebrate its fortieth anniversary. The usual social interaction between two male choirs was greatly enjoyed, and as with the previous visit, the concluding concert was given at Dublin's imposing St Patrick's Cathedral. This event was recorded for subsequent transmission on S4C television.

Realising the significance of global publicity and the importance of high-tech communication, Côr Meibion Pontarddulais had for some time operated its own website. In the autumn of 2006, it was given a complete makeover with the help of Aurora IT Solutions Ltd. It continues as a valuable resource for details of the choir's activities and achievements, its musical and administrative personnel, patrons and sponsors, and has a growing archive of photographs. Its 'Guestbook' feature has attracted countless messages of greetings and congratulations, and the area for members only, appropriately restricted by password, is an invaluable means of speedy and effective dissemination of information. It is another example of the choir's professionalism, forward-looking attitude and its willingness to embrace new and innovative ideas. The online shop linked to the website is a convenient way of purchasing a selection from the vast array of recordings made by the choir over the years. The website has attracted well over a million 'hits'.

David Last was only the choir's third principal accompanist since 1973. He had given unstinting support to Clive Phillips from the time of Noel Davies's resignation in 2002. He had shouldered considerable responsibility in concerts, broadcasts and notable competitive victories, and so it was with sadness and regret that the choir learned of his intention in 2007 to move on. His departure was nevertheless understandable, as he had been invited to become the musical director of the Dowlais Male Choir, thus realising his personal ambition to conduct a male choir with its own long and distinguished history. There was no obvious successor, so the search began for a musician of proven quality. Once again, Côr Meibion Pontarddulais was able to attract an outstanding practitioner. And for the first time in its history, the choir's principal accompanist was to be a lady.

A native of Cumbria, Rachel Attwell had come to Wales in order to study at the Royal Welsh College of Music and Drama, where she graduated with first class honours, winning several prestigious prizes in the process. She had gained a postgraduate scholarship to London's Guildhall School of Music and Drama and had won the National Eisteddfod Accompaniment Prize twice. At the time of her appointment with Côr y Bont, Rachel was the staff accompanist for the woodwind department of the Royal Welsh College of Music and Drama, where she also taught piano at the college's Junior Department. This was a very fine musical pedigree indeed, and her appointment a notable coup for Côr y Bont. An assistant accompanist was also appointed at this time, and the young Ysgol Gyfun Gŵyr pupil, Anna McGlinchey, performed with the choir in several concerts before her eventual departure to study music at Churchill College, Cambridge. Occasionally deputising for organist John Davies, the choir was also indebted to Huw Smitham for his contribution in concerts from time to time. With a strong background in male choral singing, he was the founder conductor of the Neath Male Choir. In terms of numbers this was the strongest musical team in the history of Côr y Bont, and it certainly wasn't lacking in quality either.

Whilst underlining the main events in the choir's history, it is worth recalling and reiterating the regular timetable of concerts, the nature of which had been established from the beginning of the 1960s and had been maintained over the years. Thus in 2007, local performances were given for example in Gorseinon, Skewen and Mumbles, with the choir also travelling considerably farther afield to Stratford-upon-Avon, Lincoln and Redruth in Cornwall. There were, however, two particular highlights in the choir's itinerary of that year. The first was another tour of the United States of America, on this occasion visiting Pennsylvania, Washington and New York in October.

As with other previous overseas visits, this tour had been meticulously planned years in advance, both in terms of administration and musically too. The comparatively newly established team of senior choir officials were more than competent in their preparations and could, in any case, if need be, turn to experienced personnel from the past who were still active and enthusiastic choristers. In terms of the logistical arrangements everything ran like clockwork, with priceless co-operation from stateside co-ordinators Jerry Williams, Ted Fruchey, George C Horwatt, and Hywel Davies, a former chorister from the early days. Musically, there was an awareness of the significant connection between Wales and Pennsylvania, through composers such as Joseph Parry and Daniel Protheroe, both of whom had spent a significant part of their professional lives in the American state. There was hardly a need to re-introduce their music into the choir's repertoire, because Parry's 'Myfanwy' and Protheroe's 'Nidaros', for example, were omni-present. A new CD, *God Bless America* was recorded prior to travelling, with a commercial eye on sales during the tour, and included favourites that were sure to appeal to those of Welsh descent, as well as popular American songs. As it transpired, the supply of discs quickly sold out, with concert patrons clambering for more through the choir's website shop.

An early morning start from Pontarddulais to Heathrow on 12 October was necessary in order to connect with the Virgin Atlantic flight to Newark Airport, New York. The ensuing coach journey from New York to Scranton proved to be a somewhat tedious affair with the choir arriving at their hotel close to midnight. Their opening concert was within twenty hours of their arrival. The choir's visit was an opportunity for the people of Scranton and the surrounding area to revisit its own cultural heritage, so strongly influenced by Welsh emigrants. After all, Carbondale had hosted literary and musical competitions, based on the principles of the eisteddfod as far back as 1850. This had led to a significant choral legacy both from a perspective of artistic quality and in terms of the number of participants. In 1893 the 260 strong Scranton Choral Union had taken first prize at the Chicago World's Fair choral competition, the returning victors greeted by thousands as their specially festooned train arrived at Lackawanna Station. How appropriate it was that the old, magnificent station building had by now evolved into the splendid Scranton Radisson Hotel, briefly to serve as accommodation for Côr Meibion Pontarddulais.

The first concert, organised by the St David's Societies of Northeastern Pennsylvania was given at the Lackawanna College's Mellow Theatre in Scranton, and was a resounding success, the choir members now rejuvenated following the tiring journey of the previous day. Travelling with the choir as a guest artiste was the young Carmarthenshire born baritone, Gary Griffiths, then a student at London's Guildhall School of Music and Drama. With several prestigious singing prizes already to his name, his high quality performances complemented those of the choir admirably.

On the following day, St Stephen's Episcopal Church, Wilkes-Barre, was the splendid venue for a Cymanfa Ganu, an event that once again emphasised the important links between Wales and this part of Pennsylvania. The occasion was organised and sponsored by 'The Welsh Cultural Endeavor of Northeastern Pennsylvania' and drew a capacity congregation, not only to sing the well known Welsh hymns, but also to listen to interspersed performances by Côr Meibion Pontarddulais. The guest conductor had been brought over all the way from Wales, and was no stranger to Côr y Bont. The dynamic and charismatic Alun Guy was no stranger to Wilkes-Barre either, as he had conducted there on three previous occasions. His inspired conducting, supported by Mark E Laubach's mastery of the huge four manual Austin-Skinner-Berghaus pipe organ, resulted in a never to be forgotten paean of praise, a spiritually uplifting experience for all those present. Côr y Bont had recently commenced compiling a list of honorary patrons by invitation. Members of this small select group all had close, albeit differing, connections with Pontarddulais and its famous choir. The list comprised Shân Cothi, Gareth Glyn, the Rt. Hon. Peter Hain MP, Edwina Hart AM, Brian Hughes, Dennis O'Neill, Eirian Owen, Garry Owen and Huw Tregelles Williams. Following the Wilkes-Barre Cymanfa Ganu, Alun Guy was delighted to accept the choir's invitation to join this noble fellowship.

Originally a Moravian settlement, Bethlehem, Pennsylvania, had built its reputation on the large scale manufacturing of steel. How strikingly similar these areas of the USA were to industrial south Wales – sadly similar too in the decline of those industries. There were also cultural similarities, particularly so in terms of music-making, for it was in Bethlehem that the first American performance of Bach's B minor Mass had been given in 1900. The venue for Côr Meibion Pontarddulais's next concert of the tour was Bethlehem's First Presbyterian Church, a building with a justified reputation for its fine acoustics. The concert was another resounding success, with the choir long acquainted with the customary American 'standing ovations'.

There were the usual opportunities on tour for sightseeing and learning more of the host nation's history. Before leaving the Scranton area the choristers took a train ride on the Tioga Central Railroad to witness the rich autumnal colours of the Appalachian forests, and a visit to a mining museum and coal pit had obvious echoes of home for several choir members. On the journey from the Scranton area to Washington the choir visited historic Gettysburg, with the tour itinerary booklet, meticulously prepared and distributed to all choristers, containing a succinct résumé of the story of the battlefields. The first full day at Washington afforded the opportunity of a leisurely tour of the city's large number of significant landmarks.

The choir's concert in the capital was organised by the St David's Welsh-American Society of Washington, and was held in the Gothic revival Church of the Epiphany, a building that had once housed a hospital for the wounded of the Civil War. The choir and Gary Griffiths were joined on this occasion by local mezzo soprano Catrin Rowenna Davies, daughter of Hywel Davies, mentioned earlier as one of the tour's main organisers, and former choir member. It was forty years since he had left south Wales in order to pursue a career with the World Bank. One listener, later posting a notice on the internet, wrote of the choir's performance as, 'World class – when they cut loose, the volume was visceral'.

For the final leg of the tour, travelling via Philadelphia to see the Liberty Bell, the choir headed for New Jersey and a concert of historical significance at the New York City Central Labor Council. Peter Hain, then Secretary of State for Wales, and newly installed as one of the choir's honorary patrons, had prepared a message for inclusion in the tour's concert programmes, and had written:

> Earlier this year I paid a visit myself to New York to mark the bicentenary of the Abolition of the Slave Trade Act. As part of the visit I was delighted to be able to host a commemorative reception with the son of human rights campaigner and son of an escaped slave, Paul Robeson. As 2007 marks fifty years since he made his historic transatlantic telephonic link to the South Wales Miners' Eisteddfod in Porthcawl, it was a great honour to have Paul Robeson Jr at the event. We were also

entertained by the New York Labor Chorus who themselves descended from slaves and are involved in the trade union movement. The link up with the Pontarddulais Male Choir will be quite something, mixing the passion of Wales with the passion of New York.

Founded in 1991, the Labor Chorus had performed at demonstrations, picket lines, union halls, school campuses as well as at the United Nations, singing music of social protest and from the traditions of gospel, jazz and folk music. Their stated aim of wishing to reflect, 'the rich diversity of cultures around the world that are facing struggles to exist with dignity, justice and respect', had a familiar ring about it. There were echoes here of the historical hardships faced by so many in the south Wales valleys of the past. There was also an affinity with the objectives of the Llangollen International Eisteddfod of enabling a celebration of cultures and traditions of countries across the world. The concert would be a meeting of like-minded people, and at the very last moment there would be the bonus of having Peter Hain himself as a member of the audience. Visiting New York once more on official business, he took the opportunity to support the event, giving a short opening address. Such was the rapport between the choirs, and the musical success of the concert, that plans were immediately hatched to bring the New York choir to Wales.

On the final day of the tour, there was just enough time to visit Ellis Island and the Statue of Liberty before returning to Newark airport for the flight home. As tradition dictated there were impromptu performances both at the departure lounge and on the aircraft itself, where no other passengers seemed at all irritated that it was three o'clock in the morning!

If the American tour was the first of two highlights in the 2007 calendar, the second, though different and considerably shorter, exuded its own particular kudos, and related to another of the choir's recently installed honorary patrons. The choir had never in its history accepted an invitation to perform on the day immediately following its annual concert, but 2007 was to be different, and with good cause. The annual concert itself had been a lively affair with guests 'Black Voices', the Birmingham based vocal quintet who had last appeared with the choir in 1993, and the ebullient Welsh tenor, Aled Hall. Choir members could normally look forward to the following Sunday as a time for relaxation and recharging batteries, but their presence was required at the Wales Millennium Centre in Cardiff. The glittering occasion was a Royal Gala Career Tribute to the distinguished international tenor, Dennis O'Neill. Ostensibly doubling as a sixtieth birthday celebration, most members of Côr y Bont realised that such a party was a few months premature. Dennis, of course, was a native of Pontarddulais, who was in his early teens when the young male choir began establishing itself. He had appeared with the choir on countless occasions in the past, both at home and abroad, and now he had invited them to join him and a galaxy of operatic stars for a Gala Concert in the presence of HRH The Duchess of Gloucester. The event was also to serve as a fund raising boost for St John Ambulance in Wales, for which Dennis was an ambassador. It was a unique occasion if only for the veritable array of operatic talent appearing on one stage. It was of course a reflection of the esteem in which this great singer was held by his fellow professionals across the world that so many had accepted an invitation to perform. International stars included Susan Bullock, Nuccia Focile and Sara Fulgoni, with Welsh representatives including Jason Howard, Della Jones and Shân Cothi. There were also performances by fine young singers studying at the Cardiff International Academy of Voice, newly established by Dennis O'Neill, with choral contributions by Côr Caerdydd and Serendipity as well as Côr Meibion Pontarddulais. Last, but certainly not least, the host of talent was led by Dame Kiri Te Kanawa, one of Dennis O'Neill's greatest friends and operatic colleagues. Côr Meibion Pontarddulais, and the many supporters who had travelled with the choir were able to recall with affection the annual concert of 1972 where, as a young singer destined for great things, Kiri Te Kanawa had appeared as a guest artiste. That occasion was within months of her sensational debut as the Countess in Mozart's *Le Nozze di Figaro* at the Royal Opera House, Covent Garden. The concert at the Millennium Centre was a fitting tribute to one of Wales's greatest singers, and several programmes of the evening's highlights were broadcast as part of S4C's Christmas and New Year season.

Now in its forty-seventh year, the choir had become used to a relentless momentum that carried it through its demanding schedule of rehearsals and performances. Success had followed success, and it would have been easy to ignore certain issues with the engagement diary full for the next few years. However, in common with other male choirs, Côr Meibion Pontarddulais had been concerned about recruitment for some time. We shall return to this theme in a later chapter, but it is worth noting here that choir officials at this time conducted what was called, with a considerable degree of dry humour, an 'Age Concern Survey'. As noted in the opening chapter, during its first year of existence the choir had grown to over ninety members with an average age of 26. The new survey showed that those two digits had been reversed, and the average age was now 62. A more detailed examination of the figures indicated that over a third of the choristers were over the age of seventy, and particularly alarmingly, only 6 per cent were under the age of forty. It was an issue that would need to be addressed.

The uncompromising pace continued into 2008, a year

that heralded a mixture of the new and the familiar for the choir. Like his predecessor, Clive Phillips was adamant that preparation for competition, with its meticulous attention to fine detail was a means of honing the choral machine to perfection. The discipline involved not only polished the competition repertoire, but also had obvious spin-offs for strengthening general choral technique, and the quality of all performances. The National Eisteddfod was visiting Cardiff, and the Bont would be aiming for their fifteenth win.

There were a number of choristers who could claim to have sung at all previous fourteen victories. Indeed there was a small group who had given unbroken service to the choir from the very beginning, a period of forty-eight years. This was a remarkable achievement, and one which the choir was very keen to acknowledge. In special presentations on 25 June 2008, the choir's president conferred honorary life memberships on John Thomas, William Thomas, Dilwyn Williams, Mydrim Davies and Donald Evans. Alun Davies was another founder member honoured on that evening, although he had been installed as a life member years earlier, and was now one of the Choir's life vice presidents in recognition of his outstanding service to the choir. The evening was also tinged with sadness, as those present recalled that another founder member, Brynley Jenkins, had been similarily honoured before his passing, only a few days previously.

The disappointments of Ammanford in 1970 and Neath in 1994, when only Côr Meibion Pontarddulais competed at the National Eisteddfod, were not to be repeated at Cardiff. Far from it, because seven choirs had entered, one more than in the epic battle at Swansea in 1964. Furthermore, all seven had achieved success at previous Nationals. In order of appearance they were Côr Meibion Maelgwn, Côr Meibion Pontarddulais, Côr Meibion Llanelli, Côr Meibion Pen-y-bont ar Ogwr, Côr Meibion y Brythoniaid, Côr Meibion y Traeth and Côr Meibion Dyfnant. The Eisteddfod was still experimenting somewhat with its categories of choral competitions, so on this occasion the major players were in the competition for over 45 voices. Choirs were required to perform a programme of up to fifteen minutes length, to include one test piece – Willy Richter's 'Creation'. The test piece proved something of a leveller, as it made no great demands on choral technique, nor on the interpretive powers of the various musical directors. An experienced practitioner in the world of male choirs, Richter had known very well the kind of sounds and effects that would appeal – at least in a superficial sense. There were powerful and convincing performances of the piece by most choirs. Côr y Bont had reverted to relying on familiar though challenging pieces to make up their complete programme. Their performance of the Mathias 'Gloria' was once again commended for its musical integrity and the panel of adjudicators, Pat Jones, Richard Elfyn Jones and Helena Braithwaite, praised the choir for its tenderness and well-shaped phrasing in interpreting 'Nos o Haf'. The audience sensed that this was a closely fought contest, with performances of high quality by all seven choirs. Who had achieved the necessary consistency in their performance of all pieces? Côr y Bont triumphed yet again with their fifteenth win at the National, their fourth win in six years under the direction of Clive Phillips. It is worth noting also, that such was the dedication of accompanist Rachel Attwell, that she had actually postponed her honeymoon until the competition was over. The wedding had taken place only a week before the Eisteddfod, with the choir providing entertainment at the reception. Husband Luie, originally from Portugal, had become one of the choir's greatest fans, and the accompanist was now to be known as Rachel Ramos.

Meanwhile, the list of distinguished honorary patrons was growing, and following an appearance with the choir as a guest artiste in the annual Noel Davies Memorial Concert, the delightful Elin Manahan Thomas gladly accepted the invitation and was promptly added to the list. Another local hero, Pontarddulais born and bred, rugby union wing wizard Ieuan Evans, was also delighted to accept the accolade at this time. There was an addition to the music team in 2008 with the appointment of Rhiannon Williams-Hale as associate accompanist. Once again the choir was fortunate in attracting a talented musician to a key post, further strengthening what was already a formidable team. She had already gained considerable experience as accompanist of the Treorci and Bridgend Male Choirs, and now looked forward to her work with Côr y Bont.

The close association between Pontarddulais and the Swansea Festival of Music and the Arts was noted in the opening chapter. Notably, T Haydn Thomas's Pontarddulais Choral Society had performed there on countless occasions, particularly in the 1950s. Now, with the festival celebrating its sixtieth anniversary, it was appropriate that the Pontarddulais connection was to be revived, this time with the appearance of Côr Meibion Pontarddulais. It was to be a memorable occasion as the choir shared the platform with the Estonian National Male Choir. The concert was an exciting mix of music from Wales and Estonia, with the two choirs combining to sing the hymn tune 'Llanfair', and the foundations of the Brangwyn Hall shaking under the remarkable power of the overall sound. This was Côr y Bont at its very best, reflecting the natural confidence of the singers as they shared an unique experience with the world's only fully professional male choir. Two evenings later, members of Côr y Bont sat back and listened to the Estonian Choir with the BBC National Orchestra of Wales give the first performance in Wales of Stravinsky's rarely performed opera-oratorio *Oedipus Rex*. Though this was unfamiliar territory for the Bont, another piece on the programme, Schubert's 'Song of the Spirits over the Waters', was particularly well known to them.

Television audiences have been measured in millions for decades. With the proliferation of channels over recent years, viewing figures have no doubt been diluted. But what of radio? Every Sunday morning, the Radio 4 programme, *Morning Worship*, regularly attracts an audience of some two million listeners. It is one of the most popular of all radio programmes. On 9 November 2008 the live broadcast at eight o'clock in the morning came from St Michael's Church, Pontarddulais. Not only was it Remembrance Sunday, but there was also added significance in that 2008 commemorated the ninetieth anniversary of the ending of the First World War. Vicar John Walters, leading the service, was joined by members of the church congregation; Canon Patrick Thomas of Carmarthen gave the address, and Côr Meibion Pontarddulais contributed several musical items. Typical of the reaction was one message posted on the Guestbook section of the choir's website by the conductor of Glasgow's Clydebank Male Voice Choir, who wrote, 'I congratulate your choir on a splendid contribution. I listen to this broadcast most Sundays, and can't remember ever before hearing the music provided solely by a men's choir.'

No doubt recalling that it was Côr Meibion Pontarddulais that had entertained the Millennium Stadium crowd before the opening match of the successful 2005 Grand Slam campaign, the Welsh Rugby Union now issued the choir with another invitation. The occasion was one of the biggest games of the autumn international series, with Wales once more hosting the great New Zealand All Blacks. Côr y Bont joined forces with the Regimental Band of the Royal Welsh to lead the singing. This was the famous match when having completed the *haka*, the New Zealand team were completely bewildered at seeing the Welsh players remain perfectly still, staring back at them. It was an eerie stand-off, and it took some time for the referee to persuade players from both sides that they had actually come there to play rugby! Alas, the Welsh success of 2005 was not to be repeated, and the All Blacks ran out comfortable winners.

As 2008 drew to a close, it was time for another annual concert at the Brangwyn Hall, and on this occasion the choir was joined, according to tradition, by two operatic soloists in soprano Gail Pearson and tenor Rhys Meirion. However, in this particular 'Annual' a young instrumentalist was to steal the show. Seventeen-year-old Neath born cellist Steffan Morris had been a pupil at Ysgol Gyfun Ystalyfera before taking up a place at the Yehudi Menuhin School in 2004. With a mix of pieces demanding dazzling virtuosity on the one hand, and considerable musical sensitivity on the other, he mesmerised the audience with his remarkable skill.

The choir's diary for 2009 was as full as ever with local concerts and performances further afield, though it is fair to say that much time and energy was now being spent on planning and preparing for the fiftieth anniversary celebrations. However, several of the year's concerts had special resonances. In January Côr y Bont combined with old friends and rivals, Côr Meibion Llanelli, in an evening at the Brangwyn Hall appropriately entitled 'Comrades in Arms'. Guests on this occasion were the young up and coming Carmarthen soprano Rhian Mair Lewis, and one of Wales's favourite amateur singers, Richard Allen, who had himself years earlier been a stalwart of Côr y Bont's top tenor section. Re-emphasising the versatility of the choir, there was also a return to the world of pop music, when in February backing tracks were recorded for the reality television star Rhydian Roberts's forthcoming concert tour of the United Kingdom.

A completely different highlight was the invitation to perform as part of the 700th anniversary celebrations at St Botolph's Church in Boston, Lincolnshire. One of the largest parish churches in England, its tower, and often the actual church itself, is popularly refered to as the 'Boston Stump', and its fine acoustics are acknowledged far and wide. It was another prestigious venue that Côr y Bont could add to its already extensive list.

The year's Noel Davies Memorial Concert was dedicated to the Pontarddulais Brass Band, celebrating a century of brass band music-making in the town, and the evening of brass and voices, with its unique local flavour, was enjoyed by a capacity audience.

In July, the choir had the opportunity of welcoming their old friends, the New York City Labor Chorus, to Gorseinon's Ebenezer Chapel. The two choirs had combined for a concert on the New York leg of Côr y Bont's tour of the eastern United States in 2007. Ebenezer Chapel, often described as Côr y Bont's spiritual home, was commemorating its 100th Anniversary and the proceeds of the evening were donated to the church. In September, Morriston's splendid Tabernacle Chapel was the venue for a concert in aid of the Tŷ Olwen Hospice. Once again the choir was joined by one of their Honorary Patrons, Elin Manahan Thomas, together with husband, baritone Robert Davies. After further recordings for radio and television, it was time for another annual concert at Swansea's Brangwyn Hall, with Elin and Bob again joining the choir as guest artistes. The disappointment at violinist Amir Bisengaliev's absence because of visa problems was tempered by the astonishing playing of piano virtuoso, John Lenehan, whose performance of the complete transcription of Gershwin's *Rhapsody in Blue* enraptured the audience.

Each calendar year ended for the choir with its contribution, as one of the town's musical organisations, to the popular annual carol concert organised by Côr Glandulais at the town's Gopa chapel. And then Côr Meibion Pontarddulais had reached the threshold of its fiftieth anniversary.

5

Y CÔR, Y GYMRAEG A CHYMREICTOD

Ond wedyn eu gweld nhw,
Ddynion, yn eu siwtiau yn lân ar lwyfan –
....
Eu gweld nhw ar lwyfan
A'u hwynebau'n myfyrio'r gân,
Eu llygaid yn astud
A grym eu cerdd –
Yn dangnefedd, yn orfoledd, neu'n alar –
Yn fflam drwy'r neuadd,
Fel einioes yn llosgi mewn diffeithwch o nos.

'Côr Meibion', Gwyn Thomas

Mae Gwyn Thomas yn gorffen ei gerdd trwy ddyfynu 'hen arweinydd' unwaith eto yn profi gwefr côr meibion yn canu, ac yn dweud o ganlyniad, 'Mi wn mai Duw da a wnaeth ddynion'. A sawl gwaith clywyd Cymro yn hawlio mai 'Cymraeg yw iaith y nefoedd'? Beth bynnag am hynny, yn sicr bu'r iaith Gymraeg a Chymreictod yn gyffredinol yn rhan annatod o hanes Côr y Bont o'r cychwyn cyntaf.

Sefydlwyd Ysgol Gynradd Gymraeg Pontarddulais (Bryniago yw'r enw ers blynyddoedd bellach) yn ystod y 1950au. Am y tro cyntaf erioed roedd addysg cyfrwng Cymraeg ar gael i blant y dref, o leiaf i reini dan un-ar-ddeg mlwydd oed. Dyma ddyddiau'r 'eleven plus', a didolid y plant hŷn i addysg uwchradd 'fodern' neu 'ramadeg' yn ddibynnol ar ganlyniad yr arholiad. Nid oedd y naill na'r llall, na'r ysgolion preifat a fynychid gan rai, yn cynnig addysg uwchradd cyfrwng Cymraeg, ac ni wireddwyd y freuddwyd honno yn ardal gorllewin Morgannwg am flynyddoedd lawer. Felly, daeth sefydlu'r ysgol gynradd Gymraeg yn y Bont, a'r twf sylweddol a ddilynodd hynny mewn cyfleoedd addysg cyfrwng Cymraeg, yn rhy hwyr i'r bechgyn ifainc a fu wrthi'n sefydlu'r Côr Meibion yn 1960. O ganlyniad roedd dylanwad y Saesneg yn drwm arnynt, er efallai, ar rai yn fwy na'i gilydd, ond serch hynny roedd yr ymwybyddiaeth o'r Gymraeg a Chymreictod yn dal yn gadarn ymhlith llawer iawn ohonynt. Flynyddoedd yn ddiweddarach, diddorol yw tystio i nifer sylweddol o'r aelodau, yn Gymry Cymraeg ac yn Gymry di-Gymraeg, ddanfon eu plant i ysgolion Cymraeg amrywiol y fro, ac fe ddatblygodd perthynas agos rhwng Côr Meibion Pontarddulais ag Ysgol Gyfun Gŵyr, yn enwedig ym mlynyddoedd cynnar yr ysgol honno wedi ei sefydlu yn 1984.

I ddychwelyd i Bontarddulais y 1960au, yn gyffredinol roedd dylanwad yr iaith Gymraeg a'r defnydd ohoni yn dal yn gymharol gryf. Y Gymraeg oedd yr iaith gymdeithasol naturiol i drwch y boblogaeth, ac er nad oedd y capeli anghydffurfiol bellach yn eu hanterth o gymharu â'r blynyddoedd a fu, roeddent yn dal yn gadarnleoedd y Gymraeg ac yn fwrlwm o weithgareddau. Profiad arwyddocaol nifer o sylfaenwyr Côr Meibion Pontarddulais yn blant oedd mynychu gweithgareddau'r capeli ac yn arbennig yr ysgolion Sul, y 'Band of Hope' a'r cymanfaoedd canu hefyd.

Wrth sefydlu'r côr, gwelwyd dylanwad y Gymraeg o'r cychwyn cyntaf. Enw swyddogol y côr fyddai Côr Meibion Pontarddulais, gan nodi'r cyfieithiad Saesneg hefyd. Ond y fersiwn yn y Gymraeg yn unig oedd i ymddangos ar fathodyn swyddogol y côr. Gyda rhai aelodau oedd yn medru'r iaith ac eraill oedd yn ddi-Gymraeg, wrth reswm iaith weinyddol y côr o ran cyfarfodydd pwyllgor a chofnodion fyddai Saesneg. Ond o ran swyddogion, bu mwyafrif y cadeiryddion ar hyd y blynyddoedd yn Gymry Cymraeg, a phob un o'r ysgrifenyddion dros yr hanner can mlynedd, gydag ond un eithriad, yn medru'r Gymraeg, a hwythau wrth gwrs yn defnyddio'r iaith honno'n helaeth wrth gyfathrebu ag amrywiaeth o asiantaethau ar lafar ac yn ysgrifenedig. Tri llywydd fu yn hanes y côr, a phob un o'r tri yn Gymry Cymraeg. Rhoddwyd statws teilwng i'r Gymraeg ysgrifenedig mewn rhaglenni cyngerdd ac ar ddeunydd cyhoeddusrwydd amrywiol, ac ar wefan y côr hefyd pan ddatblygwyd honno yn y mileniwm newydd, ac i'r iaith lafar mewn areithiau, cyflwyniadau a digwyddiadau cyhoeddus.

Mae gosod egwyddorion ar gychwyn unrhyw fenter yn allweddol bwysig i ddatblygiadau'r dyfodol. Yn hyn o beth, nid oedd unrhyw un yn amau Cymreictod y gŵr oedd wrth y llyw, na'i ymroddiad chwaith i'r iaith Gymraeg. Cafodd Noel Davies fagwraeth yn y 'pethe' mewn cartref lle rhoddid cryn bwyslais ar ddiwylliant Cymru. Roedd ei fam, Myfanwy, yn meddu ar lais alto cyfoethog a bu'n canu gyda chôr cymysg enwog Rhydaman pan oedd yn ferch ifanc, cyn dod maes o law yn un o aelodau blaenllaw 'Côr Mawr' T Haydn Thomas ym Mhontarddulais. Eto, o ran Noel yn blentyn, Saesneg oedd cyfrwng yr addysg yn ysgol fach Pengelli'r Drain, a Saesneg hefyd oedd iaith y gwersi yn Ysgol Ramadeg y Bechgyn, Tregŵyr. Ond y Gymraeg oedd yr iaith gymdeithasol i nifer, a Chymry Cymraeg oedd y mwyafrif o ffrindiau Noel Davies yng nghyfnod ei lencyndod. Yn oedolyn, wrth fynd yn fyfyriwr i Goleg

Harlech, fel y nodwyd eisoes, daeth o dan ddylanwad rhai o Gymry Cymraeg mwyaf brwd y cyfnod – y Pennaeth Dan Harry, a'r darlithwyr ifainc Meredydd Evans a D Tecwyn Lloyd. Wedyn wrth symud i Goleg y Drindod, Caerfyrddin, cafodd Jac L Williams yn fentor ac yn ysbrydoliaeth.

Wrth iddo sefydlu a datblygu'r côr meibion, daeth i edmygu fwyfwy arweinydd enwog a deallus Côr Meibion Treorci – John Haydn Davies. Mewn dim amser tyfodd yr edmygedd hwnnw yn gyfeillgarwch agos. Bu Cymreictod cadarn John Haydn, a'i ymrwymiad i gerddoriaeth Gymreig a Chymraeg yn ddylanwadau pwysig ar Noel. Rhwng eitemau mewn cyngerdd, byddai Noel Davies yn hoff iawn o siarad â'r gynulleidfa, yn esbonio cefndir rhyw ddarn neu gyfansoddwr efallai, neu'n aml iawn fe ddywedai ryw stori ddoniol. Ar yr adegau yma byddai'n troi'n naturiol o'r Saesneg i'r Gymraeg, bron heb i'r gynulleidfa sylweddoli! Wrth reswm, Saesneg oedd cyfrwng ymarferion y côr ond, yn ddiddorol, pan fyddai'n colli amynedd, ac yn anhapus â safon y canu, byddai'r arweinydd yn troi i'r Gymraeg. 'Is that a *fah* or a *mi*?' holai'r arweinydd. '*Fah*' atebai'r cantorion yn ffyddiog. 'Wel, canwch *fah* er mwyn dyn', meddai Noel.

Magwraeth ieithyddol wahanol a gafodd olynydd Noel Davies fel arweinydd y côr. Brodor o bentref bach Murton ym Mro Gŵyr oedd Clive Phillips, wedi ei godi'n ddi-Gymraeg, ond oherwydd ei ddalentau cerddorol, wedi dod o dan ddylanwad cerddoriaeth Gymreig a'r iaith Gymraeg o oedran cynnar iawn. Tyfodd yn gefnogwr brwd o'r byd eisteddfodol trwy ei gysylltiad â nifer o gorau, a phan ymgymerodd â'r awenau gyda Chôr Meibion Pontarddulais, ni fu unrhyw gyfaddawdu o gwbl o ran Cymreictod y côr. Cafodd yntau wrth gwrs, fel cyfeilydd y côr am ddegawd a mwy, ei ddylanwadu gan frwdfrydedd Noel Davies dros y Gymraeg a cherddoriaeth Gymreig, ac nid oedd yn syndod tystio i'w ddymuniad i barhau â'r traddodiad cyfoethog hwnnw.

Yn allweddol i Gymreictod y côr yw ei berthynas gyda'r Eisteddfod Genedlaethol. I raddau helaeth, yr Eisteddfod wrth gwrs oedd magwrfa'r corau meibion dros y ganrif a hanner ddiwethaf. Mae'n wir y gellir olrhain hanes datblygiad corau o'r math i gyfnod cynharach eto mewn hanes, a bu dylanwadau eraill pwysig yn ogystal â'r Eisteddfod. Ni ellir gwadu dylanwad cryf y capel ar ddatblygiadau corawl yn gyffredinol, yn arbennig corau cymysg ond, yn ei hanfod, y llwyfan eisteddfodol oedd un o'r dylanwadau mwyaf arwyddocaol ar gorau meibion. Yn eironig serch hynny, o ran yr Eisteddfod Genedlaethol ei hun, Seisnig a Saesneg oedd llawer o elfennau'r ŵyl 'fodern' yn dilyn dylanwad Hugh Owen o'r 1860au ymlaen, pan oedd hunan-barch y Cymry mor isel beth bynnag yn dilyn 'Brad y Llyfrau Gleision'. Araf iawn eu dylanwad oedd ymdrechion cynyddol Cymry blaenllaw, yn arbennig o droad yr ugeinfed ganrif ymlaen, i Gymreigeiddio'r Brifwyl. O'r diwedd, conglfaen cyfansoddiad Cyngor yr Eisteddfod a dderbyniwyd yn Eisteddfod Machynlleth ym 1937 oedd y 'rheol Gymraeg', sef mai 'Y Gymraeg fydd iaith swyddogol y Cyngor a'r Eisteddfod'. Yr Ail Ryfel Byd yn anad dim oedd y prif reswm dros yr oedi mewn gweithredu'r rheol honno'n llawn, ond o Eisteddfod Caerffili ym 1950 ymlaen, Cymraeg oedd iaith holl weithgareddau'r Eisteddfod. I aelodau ifainc Côr Meibion Pontarddulais felly, ar gychwyn eu hantur yn y 1960au, Cymraeg oedd unig iaith yr Eisteddfod Genedlaethol fel y gwyddent hwy amdani. Felly roedd hi hefyd pan oeddent yn cystadlu fel rhan o gôr cymysg y Clwb Ieuenctid yn y 1950au. Roedd yr ymrwymiad â'r Eisteddfod Genedlaethol, a honno'n ŵyl gwbl Gymraeg, yn llwyr a chadarn.

Trafodwyd llwyddiannau anhygoel Côr Meibion Pontarddulais yn yr Eisteddfod Genedlaethol yn llawnach eisoes ym mhenodau blaenorol y gyfrol hon. Serch hynny, mae'n werth pwysleisio eto y teyrngarwch a ddangosodd y côr, Noel Davies a Clive Phillips i'r Eisteddfod ar hyd y blynyddoedd. Mae'n annhebyg y gwelir unrhyw ragori ar eu record o bymtheg buddugoliaeth fel côr meibion, am beth amser os o gwbl. Yn y 'brif gystadleuaeth' fe'u trechwyd ond ddwywaith, a hynny gan Gôr Meibion Treorci, yn eu hanterth yn y 1960au dan arweiniad John Haydn Davies. Hyd yn oed ar y ddau achlysur hynny, daeth Côr y Bont yn ail agos. O 1968 yn y Barri hyd at 2008 yng Nghaerdydd, bu'r côr yn ddi-guro, gan ennill tair ar ddeg o gystadlaethau cenedlaethol yn ystod y cyfnod hwnnw. Yn ogystal â hyn, cafodd y côr y fraint o dderbyn gwahoddiadau i berfformio yng nghyngherddau sawl Eisteddfod Genedlaethol ynghyd â 'Gwyliau Cyhoeddi' cysylltiedig yn y gogledd a'r de.

Yn ganolog i'w hymroddiad i gerddoriaeth Gymreig a Chymraeg oedd repertoire y côr. Nid yn unig yr oedd rhwydd hynt iddynt gynllunio rhaglenni cyfan o gerddoriaeth Cymru, ond yn aml mewn cyngherddau a darllediadau radio a theledu canwyd yr holl ddarnau yn y Gymraeg. Gydag ond ambell eithriad, dysgwyd darnau gan bob cyfansoddwr corawl o bwys a fu'n gweithio yng Nghymru yn ystod yr hanner canrif o fodolaeth y côr. Yn eu plith roedd perfformiadau cyntaf o weithiau newydd, darnau a gomisiynwyd gan y côr ei hun, ynghyd â thorreth o drefniadau o emyn-donau ac alawon gwerin Cymraeg. Gwelwyd parodrwydd brwd y côr i rannu'r repertoire Cymraeg a Chymreig yma gyda chynulleidfaoedd ar draws y byd, gan chwarae rhan bwysig yn y broses o hyrwyddo cerddoriaeth Cymru'n rhyngwladol.

Yn wir, dros y blynyddoedd bu derbyn gwahoddiadau i ganu i Gymry alltud yn Lloegr a thramor yn bwysig i'r côr. Boed yn 'Gymdeithas Gymreig', yn 'Gymdeithas Gymraeg', yn 'Gymdeithas Cymru a'r Byd', yn 'Gymdeithas Dewi Sant' neu'n 'Gymrodorion', adeiladwyd perthynas lewyrchus rhwng y côr a chymdeithasau gweithgar tebyg o Gymry yn Lloegr megis Swindon, Birmingham, Chelmsford, Wyre

Valley, Bridgenorth, Harlow, Gillingham a Chatham yn ogystal â Chymry Llundain wrth gwrs. A thramor hefyd, cyfrannodd y côr tuag at gryfhau ymdeimlad o ysbryd gwladgarol ymhlith Cymry alltud Dublin yn yr Iwerddon; y Costa del Sol yn Sbaen; Ottawa, Kingston, Montreal, Calgary, Vernon, Vancouver a Mid Island yng Nghanada; ac Albuquerque, New Mexico, Pennsylvania a Washington yn yr Unol Daleithiau.

Hwyrach mai pwysicach na dim yw ymrwymiad yr aelodau i ganu yn yr iaith Gymraeg, yn enwedig felly o gofio'r aelodau di-Gymraeg niferus ar hyd y blynyddoedd. Cofier hefyd y dysgid pob darn ar y cof o'r dyddiau cynharaf, ac wrth berfformio'n gyhoeddus ni ddefnyddiwyd geiriau na cherddoriaeth ganddynt erioed.

Yn anffodus nid oes gennym fanylion penodol am aelodau'r côr yn y dyddiau cynnar, ar wahân i gofrestri'r cyfnod hwnnw yn rhoi enwau a chyfeiriadau ynghyd ag ystadegau presenoldeb mewn ymarferion. Anodd yw datgan yn bendant felly y ganran o'r aelodau oedd yn medru'r Gymraeg, dyweder ym mlwyddyn gyntaf bodolaeth y côr, sef 1960–61. Ond yn sgil ymatebion i'r holiadur y sonnir amdano ym Mhennod 6, gellir dweud yn bendant am aelodaeth y côr ym mlwyddyn dathlu'r hanner canmlwyddiant, bod 57 y cant ohonynt yn medru'r Gymraeg, a bod 9 y cant pellach yn ystyried eu hunain yn 'ddysgwyr' mewn ystyr gweithredol. Pan ofynnwyd i'r aelodau presennol nodi uchafbwyntiau personol yn ystod eu cyfnod gyda'r côr, roedd buddugoliaethau yn yr Eisteddfod Genedlaethol yn ymateb cyson. Ac wrth ystyried eu dyheadau ar gyfer y dyfodol, roedd parhau i gystadlu yn flaenoriaeth gyffredinol amlwg hefyd.

Yn ei gerdd 'Colli Iaith', mae Harri Webb yn cychwyn wrth restru'r colledion:

Colli'r hen alawon persain,
Colli tannau'r delyn gywrain:
Colli'r corau'n diasbedain
Ac yn eu lle cael clebar brain.

Ond fe wêl y bardd obaith hefyd o ran y Gymraeg a Chymreictod:

Cael yn ôl o borth marwolaeth
Gân a ffydd a bri yr heniaith:
Cael yn ôl yr hen dreftadaeth
A Chymru'n dechrau ar ei hymdaith.

Boed i Gôr Meibion Pontarddulais adlewyrchu gobeithion y bardd, gan barhau â'u hymrwymiad i'r iaith Gymraeg ac i gyfrannu ymhellach eto i gyfoeth diwylliant y genedl dros y blynyddoedd sydd i ddod.

6

THE CHOIR IN 2010, AND
FUTURE CHALLENGES

IT GOES WITHOUT SAYING that the Pontarddulais of 2010 is in so many ways very different from the Pontarddulais of 1960. General living standards have improved, and the old traditional industries of coal mining and the production of tinplate have all but disappeared. The M4 motorway, literally cutting its way through the Pontarddulais marshes, has, on the one hand, allowed travellers to bypass the town. On the other, though, it has been a means of facilitating an ease of travel unthinkable in the 1960s, allowing employees to commute to their places of work, often far from Pontarddulais itself. A third of the working population is involved in public administration, education & health, with another quarter working in distribution, the retail trade, hotels and catering. General population has remained stable at around 5,000, although more recently new housing estates have sprung up, attracting an influx of new residents. Three-quarters of households have at least one car, a far cry from 1960, and almost all have some form of central heating, the coal fires of yesteryear a distant memory.

The children of 2010 have no worries about the old 'eleven plus' examination. Indeed there is these days a comprehenive school complete with leisure centre situated in Pontarddulais itself, whose pupils at 16+ move on to the nearby Gorseinon Tertiary College. Welsh-medium education has flourished and the demand continues to grow. In the 2001 Census, 28 per cent of Pontarddulais citizens claimed that they could speak, read and write Welsh. Pontarddulais now has its own purpose-built library and there are so called 'outreach classes' available for those interested in developing their computer skills. There is also an active branch of the 'University of the Third Age'. Some of the town's chapels have closed, whilst others that have seen sense in rationalising and combining are continuing to testify to Christian mission. The 'Old Church' of Llandeilo Talybont on the marsh has been carefully taken down and authentically reconstructed at the unique Sain Ffagan Folk Museum in Cardiff, as it had stood in the early sixteenth century.

The shopping centre has changed, with an influence these days of so called 'niche' shops attracting clientèle from far and wide. The town is on the threshold of an exciting development with a proposed £40m retail, residential and leisure scheme, which could herald a new and thriving economic era for Pontarddulais and its environs.

Political and local government changes have been striking. A Welsh Assembly Government was a distant dream in 1960, but a reality since 1997. Pontarddulais, part of Glamorgan County Council in 1960, is now incorporated within the jurisdiction of the City and County of Swansea, having been in intervening years a part of West Glamorgan.

Fifty years has certainly testified to many changes, and yet there are certain aspects of the town's life that have continued as integral to the lives of residents. One of them undoubtedly revolves around sport, with rugby, cricket, soccer and bowls maintaining their considerable influence well into the second decade of the twenty-first century.

Culturally too, the town continues to flourish, and the strong musical tradition is maintained with considerable gusto. As well as Côr Meibion Pontarddulais itself, the village boasts two mixed choirs in Côr Glandulais and the senior citizens' choir, Cantorion Pontarddulais, as well as the female chamber choir, Lleisiau Lliw. The Town Band these days enjoys Championship Class status, and continues to go from strenth to strength.

A comparative analytical profile of Côr Meibion Pontarddulais as it was in 1960 and is now in 2010 would undoubtedly prove an interesting excercise. Unfortunately, detailed information on the choir's membership in the early years is somewhat sparse. We know, however, that most of the members in that first year of existence were young men and that the average age was twenty-six. The vast majority of them would have been from the town of Pontarddulais itself or the smaller neighbouring villages of Hendy, Llanedi, Grovesend, Pontlliw and Felindre – that is to say, the general catchment area of the Youth Club described in the opening chapter as the foundation for the subsequent development of the male choir itself. Compiling a profile of the membership in 2010 has been made easier through the choristers' excellent responses to a wide ranging questionnaire that form the basis for the remainder of this chapter.

Still boasting well over a hundred choristers, the catchment area has widened to a certain degree. Yet almost 40 per cent of the members in 2010 live in Pontarddulais itself or in the immediately neighbouring small villages. Another 40 per cent, however, travel to rehearsals from outside a radius of five miles.

Home Locations

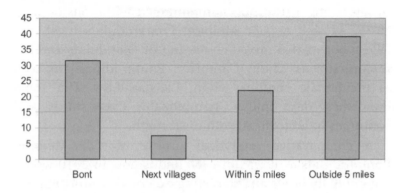

For various reasons over the fifty years, the rehearsal venue has periodically varied, but no one would quarrel with the claim that Pontarddulais Primary School at the very top end of James Street, is the choir's true home. In 1960 the building housed the Pontarddulais Secondary Modern School, and it was there that the Youth Club had met, and the club's choirs had rehearsed. It became the natural meeting place for Côr Meibion Pontarddulais from the very beginning. The school hall these days is bedecked with choir memorabilia and the splendid 'Honours Board' described in Appendix 2. On the wall is a huge version of the choir badge, fashioned in polystyrene by the Padre, Ray Hubble, at the Wildenrath RAF base, and presented to the choir during their visit there in 1979. The choir has sensibly invested in comfortable seating and a first rate piano, but tentative plans, often mooted over the years, for a permanent purpose built home have never materialised, probably because of contentment with the facilities at the school and the unwavering support of successive headteachers. The school hall is filled almost to capacity by the rehearsing choir, though countless visitors from far and wide have still managed to squeeze in to listen, at very close quarters indeed, to the magnificent choral sound. The choir's collection of Visitors' Books makes interesting reading, and show that even by 1965, the choir had welcomed visitors literally from every one of the world's continents.

An analysis of when present choristers joined the choir makes significant reading, as the graph below illustrates:

Decade of Joining

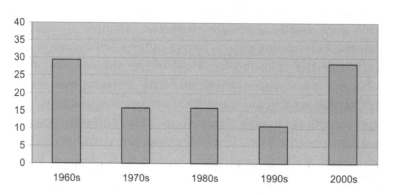

The choir has a core membership dating back to the very early days of the 1960s. In a previous chapter it was noted that a small number had been awarded life membership in 2008 in recognition of unbroken service. Many others have already proudly achieved their own personal goals of forty or twenty five years' service. Over 30 per cent of the present choristers have rejoined the choir, having temporarily left in the past, mainly due to illness, increasing family commitments or work responsibilities. Yet perhaps the most sobering statistic of all is the one pointing to continuing recruitment in the new millennium, and the realisation that over a quarter of the present membership did not sing under the founder conductor, Noel Davies, at all.

Three-quarters of the choristers have experience of singing with other choirs, with several leaving established male choirs in order to join the Bont. In responding to a question asking all members why they had joined, the expected reasons emphasising an enjoyment of singing, social camaraderie, opportunities to travel were all frequently noted. Also particularly emphasised among the reasons was 'the excitement of competing', to which we shall return later.

Numerically, vocal balance has obviously of necessity been maintained, though baritones at present slightly outumber singers in other sections. Some free transfers have been periodically negotiated between sections, a reminder that the human voice can change in terms of its range and timbre as the years go by. Most of the singers read from solfa notation, with a small minority learning new music by rote. A significant number, perhaps surprisingly, read staff notation, having learned to play different musical instruments to varying levels of competence. Collectively, at rehearsals, solfa is used when beginning to prepare a new piece.

Throughout its history, the choir has often recruited from the same families, with brothers, cousins, uncles, fathers and sons often involved at one time or another. This is the case with 21 per cent of the present membership, who have relatives either singing with the choir at present or having done so in the past. Well over a half of the choristers are actively involved with other community organisations, with a particular emphasis on sporting clubs, local politics and charity work. Almost 40 per cent are members of a chapel or church congregation, and 57 per cent are Welsh speakers with a further 9 per cent describing themselves as active learners of the language.

In the survey, each choir member was asked to note any three particular personal highlights as a chorister. Unsurprisingly many found it difficult to confine themselves to three alone. Overwhelmingly at the top of the league were the eisteddfod victories, once again emphasising the importance of competition to the present generation of Bont singers. The exhilarating experience of winning at Llangollen and at the National Eisteddfod was incomparable, though the exploits of the choir on overseas tours also rated highly. This section of the survey, apart from eliciting responses on competitions and foreign visits, also threw up a large number of other 'personal highlights'. Performances at prestigious concert halls and cathedrals were noted by many, as was 'my first annual concert'. Some were striking in their succinct simplicity – 'singing such wonderful music', whilst others were poignantly touched by a degree of sadness – 'Noel Davies's last concert'.

Asked to name their three favourite pieces from the choir's repertoire, there were once again complaints about the impossibility of confining the choice to three only. There were generic responses ranging from the erudite, 'any operatic chorus by Verdi' to the tongue in cheek, 'anything ending in a big Amen'! Though there were no runaway favourites, Cherubini's *Requiem* scored highly as did Daniel Protheroe's 'Nidaros' and Max Bruch's setting of Psalm 23. Not meant as a popularity survey, the results did however lead to some interesting conclusions. In all, over eighty pieces of music were mentioned, encompassing all styles and periods, and reflecting the choir's repertoire from the very beginning to the present day. From the simplest of folk songs to the most complex of contemporary music – they were all there.

The questionnaire also canvassed views on how the choir should move forward over the next five years, and two themes were particularly prevalent in the responses. The first was a fierce determination to maintain high standards of performance. The second indicated a deep-seated concern about the challenge of recruiting young men to the choir ranks. It comes as no real surprise that over 70 per cent of choir members are now retired. Over the fifty years, members' occupations have included a rich mix of the professional, managerial and technical, as well as those of the manually skilled and partly skilled. Jobs, background and social status have counted for nothing. A singing voice and the enthusiasm and commitment to use it to the best of one's ability has meant everything. Still, in 2010 only some 30 per cent of members are in full-time employment, and this of course underlines the choir's age profile, and the realisation that attracting younger singers is crucial for the continuing success of the choir. No organisation of fifty years standing, musical or otherwise, can really escape the clutches of this particular issue. The stark reality of the following graph is telling:

Age

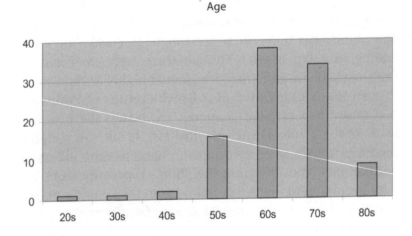

Ironically, recruitment, *per se*, is not really an issue. As shown above, the choir has continued to attract new members in significant numbers over recent years, and unusually, in terms of present day Welsh male choirs, still boasts a singing compliment of well over a hundred voices. However, the new influx, with few exceptions, has tended to be the recently retired, now with sufficient time to devote to the schedule of a particularly busy choir. At the same time, concerns about attracting recruits is nothing new, and was an issue actively addressed periodically by the choir's music staff and its officers from the 1980s onwards. Publicity drives and 'open rehearsals' were techniques used even when the choir was celebrating its twenty-fifth anniversary. Now, though, statistics underlined that young men very rarely joined. Speaking generally, some social commentators have sceptically denounced the younger generation as being disinterested in anything to do with cultutre and the arts, arguing that singing, to use modern parlance, was not seen as 'cool'. However, some significant events in the world of Welsh choral music towards the end of the first decade of the twenty-first century was to prove their thesis was absurdly flawed.

Last Choir Standing was a BBC television talent show broadcast during peak Saturday evening viewing slots in July and August 2008. The programme's aim was to discover the UK's 'favourite choir'. Applications were received initially on tape from around a thousand choirs, sixty of which were then invited to audition live. Twenty seven received callbacks, with fifteen eventually selected to perform in three rounds of studio heats. Choirs were gradually eliminated through a process of viewer votes. What began as an United Kingdom phenomenon ended firmly as a Welsh one, and at the same time the cynics who had argued that youngsters had no interest in singing were silenced. Winners were the young south Wales-based male choir Only Men Aloud with the youth choir of north Wales's Ysgol Glanaethwy as runners up. It was a competition far removed from the tradition of the Eisteddfod. A cursory glance at the repertoire performed by almost all choirs showed a preponderence of 'pop' music arrangements and songs from the shows, with choreography a vital part of the performance. Indeed a 'safety track' was prepared for performances that included choreography or movement, when a pre-recording of the choir's performances in a sound studio before each show was mixed in with their live studio performances during those specific pieces. Traditionalists may not have been impressed, but the programme certainly succeeded in raising the profile of choral singing, with the final result emphasising that many young people in Wales remained enthusiastic members of choral groups, achieving remarkably high standards of performance.

The supremacy of youthful Welsh choristers in that particular competition really came as no surprise. Both choirs had achieved remarkable successes, particularly within Wales, before the *Last Choir Standing* series. However, they were not alone. In S4C's 2009 *Côr Cymru* competition, it was the youngsters of Ysgol Gerdd Ceredigion, winners of the children's choir category, who actually took the overall prize – a truly remarkable achievement in a field of top class adult choirs. Equally significant, the youth category comprised a galaxy of first rate choirs, and it was a male choir that triumphed – and it too was from Ysgol Gerdd Ceredigion. Standard of choreography was not of particular relevance in this competition, and repertoire, although varied, was somewhat removed from the lighter fare of *Last Choir Standing*. Traditionalists were more content, but were unprepared for the shock that was to come only a few months later.

Successes of great Welsh choirs, including Côr Meibion Pontarddulais, in the male choir competition at the Llangollen International Eisteddfod have been discussed in a previous chapter. Victory there is still viewed by many as the ultimate accolade. The result in 2009 shook the world of male choirs, with the young men of Ysgol Gerdd Ceredigion winning, and in the process relegating the fine Westminster Chorus of California into second place, and the famous Côr Meibion Rhosllannerchrugog into third.

So, what was the significance of these developments with regards to the future of Côr Meibion Pontarddulais? One thing was certain – young Welsh men still sang, often in male choirs and invariably to a high standard. Why then could established choirs such as the Bont not attract them? And what, if anything, could be done to reverse the trend? These are complex questions which many choirs have chosen to ignore in the vain hope that the tide will turn, somehow of its own accord. On the other hand, members of Côr Meibion Pontarddulais acknowledged the challenge, and, particularly as they approached the fiftieth anniversary, set about exploring possible solutions.

Initial discussions centred around ideas that had been tried with varying success in the past. Marketing ploys such as leaflet drops and press advertisements were revived, as were personal approaches to individuals who had shown an interest in the past. The choir website was given another makeover, and members were encouraged to 'bring a friend' on a specific rehearsal evening. As some smaller local male choirs declined, some of their members now looked for a new choral 'home'. New members were indeed consequently recruited and, between September 2009 and the annual concert towards the end of November, fourteen new members had joined the ranks of Côr y Bont. However, the overall average age of choir members was little affected.

Leigh Orpheus, a male choir from Essex, facing similar challenges, had formulated an interesting structured plan, which they decided to share with representatives of south Wales choirs at a specially convened 'Come and Sing Seminar' in Neath in February 2009. Their 'Come and Sing' project involved bringing together a substantial group of new singers to form a training choir that after a period of several months' rehearsals would be incorporated within Leigh Orpheus itself. The ploy was non-threatening as no-one would be thrown in at the deep end. In rehearsals, each section was to be supported and mentored by two experienced singers from the Leigh Orpheus Choir, helping to guide, enthuse and encourage. The strategy worked remarkably well, and following a sustained publicity drive a training choir of around ninety singers was formed. Ultimately, over half became full members of Leigh Orpheus, swelling its ranks to over 120 voices. The seminar at Neath attracted representatives from several south Wales male choirs, including Côr Meibion Pontarddulais, reflecting a widespread general concern regarding recruitment. The seminar certainly stimulated discussion, with agreement that the Essex choir had at least addressed a critical issue in a positive manner. However, could such a strategy simply be transplanted into an area with a proliferation of male choirs? Had the Leigh experiment succeeded because in their part of the country male choirs were few and far between?

As discussions continued within Côr Meibion Pontarddulais, three separate themes came to the fore. First, it was once again acknowledged that the choir now approaching its fiftieth birthday had initially developed from a youth group. Secondly, recent high-profile competitions such as *Last Choir Standing*, *Côr Cymru* and the Llangollen International Eisteddfod had dispelled the myth that young Welsh men no longer sang with any proficiency. And thirdly, the formation of a 'training choir' had worked for one distant English male choir. Combining these thematic strands resulted in a proposal to consider forming a new youth 'training' choir, or possibly a younger boys' choir separate from, but under the auspices of Côr Meibion Pontarddulais. It is a striking idea, which, if successful, will take time to set up and to take root. It is interesting to note that Only Men Aloud have begun to explore similar concepts with the formation of Only Boys

Aloud. At present it is too early to assess the success or otherwise of such initiatives, but they are laudable attempts to address an issue that will increase in its significance as years go by.

And with regards the future, what are the personal ambitions of the present choristers? Reflecting the title of this book, they will all undoubtedly simply say, 'Keep on singing'! As they responded to the questionnaire, highlights of the past also influenced the ambitions for the future, with overseas tours, performances at prestigious venues and television and radio broadcasts all coming high on the list. There is a continuing hunger to learn new music and increase the repertoire, maintaining the stylistic variety that has been such a feature of the choir for over fifty years. The appetite for conquering challenging works is undiminished. More than anything, perhaps, they still see themselves as a competitive choir, and there is little doubt that we shall see them again at the National Eisteddfod and at Llangollen in the future, and possibly looking further afield towards international competitive festivals. All of these aspirations reflect the fact that choristers are greatly enthused by what they do and have thoroughly enjoyed their singing over the years. Their commitment and loyalty is truly astonishing, and the punishing schedule of rehearsals, concerts, television and radio broadcasts, recordings, overseas tours and competitions continues without compromise.

Presumably, the small group of 'augmented youth choir members' who famously met on 19 October 1960 were prepared for their proposed enterprise to flounder. After all, it was speculative to say the least, and yet it was very bold. It was ambitious with that strange mix of confidence and naivety often found in those on the threshold of adulthood. In his book, *Great Welsh Voices*, Alun Guy writes of Côr Meibion Pontarddulais:

The general consensus amongst adjudicators and critics alike is that the combined voices of over a hundred members produce for this choir the best amateur choral sound not only in Wales but in Britain and beyond.

It is an accolade that those youngsters of fifty years ago would not even have dreamed of. The story has been a remarkable one, and the fiftieth anniversary is but a milestone, for the story continues. Brothers, sing on!

APPENDIX 1

Choir Membership/Aelodau'r Côr 2010

Tenor 1

Denis Baker, Mark Bowen, Clive Davies, Eifion Davies, Gareth J Davies, Tudor Davies, Roy W. Davies, Graham Francis, Peter Garrard, Barrie Glenister, David Gwynn, Nantlais Jones, Gwynfor Jones, Ronald Jones, Trevor Jones, Stewart Kangley, Roger Kenyon, Ifor Miles, Hywel Morgan, Bill Nicholls, Mike O'Neill, Malcolm Palmer, Winston Price, Gareth Thomas, Hugh Walters, Arthur Williams, David Williams

Tenor 2

Lyn Anthony, Jeremy Bayliss, Howard Berry, Bryan Davies, Gwyn Davies, Peter Davies, John Davies, John Delbridge, Denzil Edwards, Royston Hopkins, Gwynant Hughes, Brian Jones, Harry Kedward, David Keen, Melvyn Mainwaring, Peter Morgan, David Morris, Gareth Price, Kevin Roberts, Harold Rowe, Islwyn Thomas, William Thomas, Derek Washer, Noel Williams, Richard Williams, Ian Withey

Bass 1

David Daniel, David Davies, Gareth Davies, Mansel Evans, Maybery Evans, Gwyndaf Gimblet, Terry Hale, John Hardwicke, Richard Hood, David Howard-Willis, Mike John, Glyn Jones, David Jones, Gareth Jones, Les Jones, Rhidian Jones, Gwyn Jones, Douglas Mackay, Barry Moore, Ieuan Owen, Huw Philpot, Jeffrey Prangle, Gwynne Price, Hywel Rees, Graham Rees, Michael Richards, Dewi Roberts, John Thomas, Wynford Thomas, Dilwyn Williams, Wil Williams

Bass 2

William Bevan, Antony Bidder, Emyr Daniel, Cecil Davies, Alun Davies, Mydrim Davies, Roy Davies, Gary Evans, Trevor Evans, Howell Evans, Bill Griffiths, Dave Haywood, Thomas Hill, William Hobson, Spencer Howell, David James, Mansel Jenkins, Glyndwr Johnson, Tregellis Jones, Gareth Lewis, Haydn Lewis, John Mehigan, Robert Morris, Gareth Tomos, John Walters, Kenneth Wheeler, Jeffrey Young

APPENDIX 2

Roll of Honour/Rhestr Anrhydeddau

An honours board was erected in 2009 in the hall of Pontarddulais Primary School – the choir's rehearsal room. It forms part of a large display cabinet containing trophies and important momentos and artefacts from the choir's history. The honours board reads as follows:

Codwyd bwrdd anrhydeddau yn 2009 yn neuadd Ysgol Gynradd Pontarddulais – ystafell ymarfer y côr. Mae'n ffurfio rhan o gabinet arddangos sy'n dal amrediad o dlysau a chofroddion amrywiol o hanes y côr. Mae'r bwrdd anrhydeddau yn darllen fel a ganlyn:

Côr Meibion Pontarddulais

Founder / Sylfaenydd
Noel G Davies MBE, JP 1928–2003
Conductor Emeritus / *Arweinydd Emeritws*

Presidents / Llywyddion
Professor Ieuan Williams 1960–99
Noel G Davies MBE, JP 2002–03
Eric Jones 2004 –

Musical Directors / Cyfarwyddwyr Cerdd
Noel G Davies MBE, JP 1960–2002
Clive Phillips 2002 –

Principal Accompanists / Prif Gyfeilyddion
Bryan Llewellyn, Elwyn Sweeting, Eirwyn Richards,
Wyn Davies, Eric Jones, D Hugh Jones, Clive Phillips,
David Last, Rachel Attwell

Roll of Honour / Rhestr Anrhydedd
Life Vice Presidents / Is-Lywyddion Am Oes
Mrs Gwen Williams

D Alun Davies

John G P Davies JP

Life Members / Aelodau Am Oes
Noel G Davies MBE JP

John Hadyn Davies MBE

D Alun Davies

Thomas Coles

Eric Jones

John G P Davies JP

Edward Morgan JP

Clive J Phillips

D Hugh Jones

D Winston Price

Mydrim Davies

Donald Evans

Brynley Jenkins

Nantlais Jones

John Thomas

William Thomas

Dilwyn Williams

Achievements / Llwyddiannau
National Eisteddfod of Wales / Eisteddfod Genedlaethol Cymru
Winners / Enillwyr

1963	Llandudno	1965	Newtown
1968	Barry	1970	Ammanford
1972	Haverfordwest	1974	Carmarthen
1976	Cardigan	1978	Cardiff
1981	Machynlleth	1982	Swansea
1994	Neath	2003	Maldwyn
2004	Newport	2006	Swansea
2008	Cardiff		

Awarded Côr yr Wyl / Choir of the Festival

2004 Newport   2006 Swansea

Llangollen International Eisteddfod / Eisteddfod Gydwladol Llangollen

Winners / Enillwyr

2001   2004

Pantyfedwen Eisteddfod Cardigan / Eisteddfod Pantyfedwen Aberteifi

Winners / Enillwyr

1964	1970
1965	1971
1967	1972
1968	1974
1969	1976

Miners' Eisteddfod / Eisteddfod y Glowyr – Porthcawl

Winners / Enillwyr

1965	1968
1969	1976
1980	1987

Eisteddfod Pantyfedwen Pontrhydfendigaid

Winners / Enillwyr

1965   1968

APPENDIX 3

MUSIC TEAM AND CHOIR OFFICIALS

Y TÎM CERDD A SWYDDOGION Y CÔR 2010

Musical Director *Cyfarwyddwr Cerdd* – Clive Phillips

Accompanist *Cyfeilydd* – Rachel Ramos

Associate Accompanist *Cyfeilydd Cysylltiol* – Rhiannon Williams-Hale

Organist *Organydd* – John M Davies

President *Llywydd* – Eric Jones

Life Vice Presidents *Is-Lywyddion am Oes* –
John G P Davies, Alun Davies

Chairman *Cadeirydd* – John G P Davies

Vice Chairman *Is-Gadeirydd* – Gareth Lewis

Secretary *Ysgrifennydd* – Lyn Anthony

Treasurer *Trysorydd* – Bryan Davies

Ticket Officer *Swyddog Tocynnau* – Antony Bidder

Registrar *Cofrestrydd* – John Walters

Transport Officer *Swyddog Trafnidiaeth* – Gwyn Davies

Publicity Officer *Swyddog Cyhoeddusrwydd* – Gareth Tomos

Marketing Officer *Swyddog Marchnata* – John Delbridge

Social Secretary *Ysgrifennydd Cymdeithasol* – Mark Bowen

Uniforms Officer *Swyddog Gwisg* – Gareth Price

Co-opted Committe *Pwyllgor Cyfetholedig* –
Alun Davies, Winston Price

APPENDIX 4

OVERSEAS TOURS/TEITHIAU TRAMOR

1966, May–June
SWEDEN (Tranas, Växjö, Gislaved)

1973, September–October
EASTERN CANADA (Montreal, Ottawa, Kingston)

1977, May–June
EASTERN CANADA (Montreal, Ottawa, Kingston, Deep River)

1979, January
GERMANY (Wildenrath, Rheindahlen)

1980, May
GERMANY (Wildenrath, Rheindahlen, Huckelhoven)

1986, February
PORTUGAL (Lisbon, Coimbra)

1989, May
IRELAND (Dublin)

1993, October
USA (New Mexico, Colorado, Arizona)

1996, May
WESTERN CANADA (Calgary, Vernon, Vancouver, Victoria)

2001, October
SPAIN (Torrevieja, Callosa de Segura)

2003, June
JERSEY (St Helier)

2006, October
IRELAND (Dublin)

2007, October
USA (Scranton, Wilkes-Barre, Bethlehem, Washington, New York)

2010, February/March
SPAIN (Fuengirola)

APPENDIX 5

RECORDINGS/RECORDIADAU

Teldisc Extended Play
TEP 820 [1963], TEP853 [1965], TEP 857 [1966]

Gone are the days
QUA 12008 [1966] (re-released as Great Welsh Choirs, DAF 214)

How Green was my Valley
ATL 4205 [1967]

Eisteddfod Winners
MEP 1312 [1968]

Glory in th Valley
GGL [1970]

Colditz
BBC 146S [1973] (With the Band of the Welsh Guards)

The Famous Choirs of Wales
SCLP 609 [1975]

Sanctus
BRAN 1201 [1977]

Côr Meibion Pontarddulais
SAIN 1178D   [1978]

Doniau Difyr Lliw
SAIN 1166R [1980]

Consolation of Music / Cysur y Gân
SAIN 126D [1983]

Softly as I leave you
GRTTC 8 [1985] [re-released as *Great Voices from Wales* Delta CD6594] [2006]

The Sound of Silence / Sain Tawelwch
SCD 9085 [1990]

Christmas from the Land of Song
CDB 7 975722 [1991]

Famous Choirs of Wales
CDBM 2084 [1993]

The Old Rugged Cross
CDBM 355 [1995]

Songs from England, Scotland and Wales
WMCD 2002 [1996]

Welsh Male Voices Sing Gershwin
Carlton Sounds 30360 00882 [1997]

A Celebration
CDBM 552 [2002]

As Long as I have Music
PMC 1 [2005]

Songs from Wales
GRCD 124 [2006]

God Bless America
PMC 2 [2007]

From the Valleys
ABC 4800932 [2009]

Let All Men Sing
SAIN CD2625 [2010]

As well as the above recordings Côr Meibion Pontarddulais has appeared on a large number of compilations.

APPENDIX 6

The Fiftieth anniversary year

Blwyddyn Dathlu'r Hanner

Canmlwyddiant 2010

Saturday 30th January
Concert, Hope-Siloh Chapel, Pontarddulais
A concert to commemorate the reopening of renovated chapel buildings forthwith to be known as Hope-Siloh. The proceeds of this concert were shared between the chapel and the church of St Teilo.

Friday 26th February – Friday 5 March
Concert Tour to Spain
Performances were given at the *Salon Varietes* in Fuengirola (27 and 28 February) and at the Fuengirola Park Hotel (3 March). The choir attended a reception and dinner given by the local Welsh Society on St David's Day. A visit was arranged to the Alhambra Palace, Granada.

Saturday 27th March
Concert, Sacred Heart Centre, Morriston
Proceeds to the Salvation Army.

Saturday 15th May
Concert, Guildford Cathedral

Tuesday 6th July
Annual Noel Davies Memorial Concert and Fiftieth Anniversary Concert, Brangwyn Hall, Swansea
The concert celebrated music-making in present day Pontarddulais. Côr Meibion Pontarddulais were joined by Côr Glandulais, Cantorion Pontarddulais, Lleisiau Lliw, the Pontarddulais Town Band, Osian Dafydd, Adele O'Neil and Garry Owen.

Saturday 10th July
Concert, St Agnes Church, Port Talbot

Saturday 25th September
Concert, Ysgol Bro Myrddin, Carmarthen
To celebrate the 10th anniversary of Tŷ Cymorth Hospice in
Carmarthen.

Saturday 2nd October
Concert, Lincoln Cathedral

Friday 29th October
50th Anniversary Dinner Dance
At the Stradey Park Hotel, Llanelli.

Saturday 27th November
Annual Concert, Brangwyn Hall, Swansea
With guest artistes, Shân Cothi and Alfie Bowe.

Saturday 11th December
Concert, Winslow
A traditional Christmas Concert organised by the local Rotary Club.

Sunday 19th December
Christmas Carol Concert, Pontarddulais
The Annual Pontarddulais Christmas Carol Concert at Gopa Chapel
organised by Côr Glandulais.

Brothers, Sing On! is just one of a whole range of publications from Y Lolfa. For a full list of books currently in print, send now for your free copy of our new full-colour catalogue. Or simply surf into our website

www.ylolfa.com

for secure on-line ordering.

TALYBONT CEREDIGION CYMRU SY24 5HE
e-mail ylolfa@ylolfa.com
website www.ylolfa.com
phone (01970) 832 304
fax 832 782